Vagabond

Vagabond

TIM CURRY

C

CENTURY

CENTURY

UK | USA | Canada | Ireland | Australia
India | New Zealand | South Africa

Century is part of the Penguin Random House group of companies
whose addresses can be found at global.penguinrandomhouse.com

Penguin Random House UK,
One Embassy Gardens, 8 Viaduct Gardens, London SW11 7BW

penguin.co.uk

Penguin
Random House
UK

First published in the US by Grand Central Publishing 2025
First published in the UK by Century 2025
002

Book interior design by Amy Quinn

Printed and bound in Great Britain by Clays Ltd, Elcograf S.p.A.

The authorised representative in the EEA is Penguin Random House Ireland,
Morrison Chambers, 32 Nassau Street, Dublin D02 YH68

A CIP catalogue record for this book is available from the British Library

ISBN: 978–1–529–93247–8

MIX
Paper | Supporting
responsible forestry
FSC® C018179
FSC
www.fsc.org

Penguin Random House is committed to a sustainable future
for our business, our readers and our planet. This book is
made from Forest Stewardship Council® certified paper.

For Marcia and Kate

I must go down to the seas again, to the lonely sea and the sky,
And all I ask is a tall ship and a star to steer her by...

—John Masefield

Contents

Introduction

"Honey, you're the third Tim Curry to call today," she said, and hung up the phone.

It was the spring of 1976. By an extraordinary coincidence, I had recently moved into a great apartment right behind the Waverly cinema, in New York's Greenwich Village. The Waverly was the flagship of several key venues that were experiencing success with a little film called *The Rocky Horror Picture Show*, whose new life had only just taken off.

I'd been in the stage adaptation, and we'd had an extraordinary run in London and Los Angeles. But when the film was released in 1975, it had bombed rather spectacularly. Less than a year later, it was going through a sort of renaissance, due to some genius marketing and raucous audience participation.

Naturally, I was curious, however hesitant, about this new incarnation. I'd called a day ahead of time, to let them know that I was a member of the cast and to ask if they would be so kind as to reserve a few tickets for my friends and me.

"And who are *you*?" the woman asked. Her accent was rather aggressive and I caught the distinct whiff of exaggerated boredom in her tone.

"This is Tim Curry."

That was when I was informed of the previous two Tims. The receiver dinged, and the line went dead.

I stared at the phone, both bemused and irate by her response. Ultimately, my friends and I showed up anyway (with identification). We didn't wear special costumes or anything like that— I'm not inclined to do so unless it's required or earned. Luckily, as much renewed success as the show was now having, it wasn't terribly difficult to get tickets. We went in and sat toward the back of the theater. I was far more interested in viewing the spectacle than in participating, and the crowd's engagement was a true delight to behold.

Before long, people started noticing me. A group of girls came up to my seat, giggling, touched my arm or leg, then tittered as they dispersed. It was all rather surreal, especially with the film, the fevered audience participation, and the all-too-familiar music carrying on in the background.

Unintentionally, I'd created a stir among the already animated audience. About a half hour into the film, the woman from the ticket booth of the Waverly—a slightly bedraggled, very unlikely blonde—hustled down the aisle and pulled me out of my seat.

"You are an im*pos*ter," she hissed. "You *must* leave. You're a *nightmare!* And you are *not* Tim Curry *at all—you* don't even look like *him!*" She pointed at the screen, her long red fingernail trembling with emphasis.

I stood up slowly and, with a mixture of embarrassment and triumph (neither of which were particularly founded), I handed her my passport.

She snatched it, squinted at the photo, looked back at my face, then back at the passport. In the flickering light, I watched her haughty expression collapse. Speechless, she seemed to sort of melt in front of me, evoking a wicked witch who had been assaulted by a bucket of water.

Aware I was now on a stage of sorts, I steadied myself and waited for her response.

"Ohhh my God. Oh, Mr. Curry. I didn't...Please just... please sit down."

I took my passport back and gestured to my friends.

"I wouldn't dream of it!" I said, and promptly strode out of the cinema.

———

By definition—as one who has professionally pretended or masqueraded onstage, onscreen, and into a microphone—there is an argument to be made that I have been a career imposter for most of my life.

But if you ask me, there's a much better word for my vocation and identity, a word that carries me back to my earliest days.

Vagabond.

Vagabonds rove. We travel about and pick up work wherever we go. We wander, drift, stagger, wink. Reluctant to be pinned down, we're enticed by risk, restless if we linger, fueled by curiosity and a sense of wonder.

Vagabonds learn, often from a young age, that indeed time is fleeting. As is fame—a fairly worthless pursuit, really. We are less startled by life's unpredictable shifts than those who choose to remain safe and settled. We often practice our trade in varied locations.

Those of us with itinerant upbringings or similar proclivities often have no choice but to adapt and reinvent ourselves. Over and over and over again. We rely on charming exteriors and don't mind saying so, leading us to project an inflated sense of self-confidence. We feel deeply but are perhaps less inclined to express our true selves to others—because our relationships so often prove to be ephemeral.

Of course, these qualities don't apply to all vagabonds. I'm not sure they'll apply to me tomorrow. But it feels about right today.

In Shakespearean times, people of the stage were considered rogues and vagabonds. I always rather liked that. I presume that such labels came about because of actors assuming manifold identities, traveling from one town to the next in pursuit of new audiences and a bit of coin here and there. How *can* you trust somebody, or truly know somebody, who appears as a king one day and a jester the next? What does it mean when neither role is the true identity of the person, and when that very person might be gone the next day? These entertainers with ever-changing faces and varied costumes were presumed to be scoundrels, not regarded as honorable or honest members of society.

That part doesn't define me, of course.

I'm *very* trustworthy.

You believe me, don't you?

———

Over the course of my life, my vagabond blues, hopes, and highs have found their way into varied channels of expression, different creative boxes from which flashes of my real self could emerge. Through my songs. Delivered upon the stage. Exhibited on screens. Cultivated in my homes and gardens. Re-envisioned, attached to, and filtered through more voices and personas than I can recall.

Much of this book has involved returning to those characters, the ones who defined my professional life. As there is a piece of me who either exists in or understands each of the roles we'll be revisiting, surveying them together will hopefully yield a colorful, curious mosaic of who I am, beneath the cosmetics and costumes.

Looking in the rearview mirror is neither my instinct nor my preferred way of being. I'd rather get on with it and keep moving forward. I have never been one to dwell on past performances any more than is required. I do not snatch memorabilia from my films to keep it displayed around my house like glistening ashes. I find little reward lingering in nostalgia. Living gig to gig for the better (and worse) part of half a century, I have grown accustomed to appreciating and accepting lessons offered, then looking forward to the next challenge.

That's the vagabond's way.

And yet, it hasn't escaped my notice that others have jumped at the opportunity to make their own assumptions. I have been described as everything from a confounding sex symbol, to a home designer, to a rock 'n' roll singer, to an *imposter*, to the prince of Halloween, to a paralyzed tragic case, to a dead legend.

Contrary to village gossip, I am still very much alive.

So, while that remains the case, I believe it's my turn—and my privilege—to malign my own reputation.

———

Why expose myself now? After all, I'm quite comfortable in the shade, and it would be easy enough to remain there. But with time, the thought of sharing my story stayed on my mind and felt just risky enough to intrigue me as a creative pursuit. I've also developed increasing respect for the characters I've played over the course of my life, characters about whom I've spent no small amount of time answering (and avoiding) questions.

More than anything, the challenges presented to me by being alive, by the pandemic, and by sundry health issues have offered an appalling amount of time to reflect. Strewn amid those reflections has been a recurring fantastical notion: *Maybe it's time to write my story*. Before I could even finish musing about what that might mean, self-doubt had persistently reared up, chuckling malevolently: *You've got a nerve.*

I'm prone to heed that voice, which has so often intervened, posing the deceptively simple question: *Who do you think you are?*

However, as loud and obstructive as that voice has been throughout my life, generations of you (yes, *you*) have continued to flatter me with curiosity and kind attention. In doing so, you have given me permission to mute my self-deprecating instincts—or at least to hold them at bay.

Today, I am physically unable to take you on a vigorous vagabond's adventure, due to a stroke I endured in 2012 that has limited my capacity as an active tour guide. But my mind and most of my memories have remained intact, and within them exist a multitude of journeys perhaps worth sharing. Before I can no longer be bothered to recount them, I humbly invite you into my stories of living across various environments: seaside living, country living, city living; on the road, on the stage, crossing borders and blurring them, ever in a vagabond state. I've loved inhabiting most of those settings, and—with some notable exceptions—enjoy remembering the times I've had.

You should know what you're in for, however.

I'd hate to leave you dissatisfied.

Before we raise the curtains, before the elevator descends, know this:

This will not be a master class. I have stories to impart, not explicit lessons to teach. You may glean profound takeaways from where I've been, how I got there, whom I've met, what I've done, or how I finagled my way into repeatedly being cast as an irresistible villain. Even so, my words are not meant to serve as instructions on how to act, sing, become a voiceover artist, or remain resilient in the face of unforeseen physical hardship. In part, because I do not believe that I have mastered any of those things. Furthermore, since I was a young boy, I've been dubious of anyone who claims to be an authority. Far be it from me to adopt an expert's stance now.

I must also warn (or assure) you that while there are scraps of my nature in all of my characters, I am none of them. That sentence feels too ludicrously obvious to put in writing, but the distinctions between who I really am and who I've pretended to be as an actor have proven to be a source of great disappointment to some audiences. It has not caused me much personal distress, beyond the periodic necessity to deter stalkers.

Nor will this be a juicy Hollywood tell-all. Not because my moral compass won't allow it, or because I haven't had ample run-ins with juicy celebrities—but simply because I find such books immensely dull and highly susceptible to gathering dust.

I also won't be dishing out lurid details of my love affairs. I guarantee you, if it matters, that I have experienced true love, true heartbreak, and everything in between, including no small amount of wreckage. Which, naturally, helps inform who I am.

I have loved and been loved and I hope you have, too. But I'm not interested in your romances. And specifics about my affairs of the heart or the bedroom are—respectfully—none of your fucking business.

With those caveats taken care of, I sincerely hope you enjoy the escapades, illusions, and contradictions I've collected recklessly over the course of my vagabond days.

I trust you're now shivering with antici—*I'll play along; I'll SAY IT*—pation...

Let's get on with it.

Chapter One

Setting the Stage

BY ALL ACCOUNTS (MATHEMATICALLY CONFIRMED), I WAS conceived in South Africa, which bears no relevance to my life other than to add to the tally of countries my parents referred to as "home." My mother and father met in Malta, my older sister, Judy, was born in Port Said (near Cairo), and I was born in Grappenhall, a village in Cheshire, England, on April 19, 1946. Within a year of my birth, we had moved again, this time to Hong Kong.

While there, significantly before I had the capacity to protest, my mother took me to a commercial photographer, who submitted my image to a newspaper competition for the "Most Beautiful Baby in Hong Kong." I was rather cherubic at the time, with blond, wavy hair and inordinately large, blue eyes. I must have appealed to enough of the people who would vote for such a wretched contest, because I won. My mother later told me, without the slightest uptick of enthusiasm, of this ghastly honor that had been bestowed upon me. There was no reward.

We remained there for about two years. I don't have the faintest flash of memory about my tenure as the most beautiful baby in Hong Kong, nor did my sister, though she was four years older. Before long, we returned to England and slowly etched our way around the border of the isle, moving from seaside town to seaside town for the first dozen years of my life, due to my father's position in the Royal Navy.

———

Born immediately after World War II, I grew up during a very dull, strange time, an era of lingering tensions and rationing of everything from onions to stockings to expressions of joy. Even sweets were rationed, which was a devastating scarcity for a child of five or six. Postwar England, far from feeling triumphant, was a dreary place to be. I was very lucky, however, because my father's position meant that we were always deposited by the sea.

Living by the water had a huge effect on me. I believe it contributed to my craving to always live on the edge—at the cliffs and crags of the world. Being beside the sea has always stoked my imagination and fueled my curiosity about what lies beyond.

Lest you think my childhood idyllic, I did not grow up in the type of family that enjoyed jolly holidays together. But the proximity to the ocean meant that we occasionally visited places like the Isle of Wight, in the middle of the English Channel. We went there one summer, and my sister and I dressed up and performed some sort of little play that my parents were forced to endure. I remember that time specifically because my tummy became a little upset, so I was given my first long sip of Coca-Cola—a transformative sensation that I can still taste. (It's always better out of the bottle, but my mother would have put it in a glass. To her, drinking straight from a bottle would seem common. She was a snob, with very little right to be. Neither my sister nor I were, and perhaps the fact that my dad was *not* one was among the reasons we both adored him.)

We lived for short bursts of time in places like Lee-on-Solent and Portsmouth, the latter being a quite distinguished naval port. In Portsmouth, for a while we were placed in a housing development that had been funded by the navy. I liked that a lot because there were a few other kids hanging about. It was quite a bustling scene. During that time, when I was probably about eight or nine years old, I roller-skated *everywhere*, and that included my daily glide down the road, where a friend and I liked to play Monopoly. But then we moved again, and eventually settled in a quiet home on a quiet street in Plymouth.

We were partly there because my grandfather lived nearby and my mother had spent some time there growing up. We lived in a rather dull and slightly desolate flat. It had a scullery, which I had never heard of before. Our flat was on the second floor of a slightly old house. Judy had a bedroom at the far end, and I slept in what might have originally been a dining room but had later been cobbled together as a bedroom.

There was nothing on the walls, and nothing to keep one from feeling quite isolated there. My time in that home was a sad and lonely time, when I dwelled too much on feeling that this particular turn in my life was quite unfair. Judy was rarely there—she had left for boarding school when she was about twelve—and I missed her terribly.

As for the town itself, Sir Francis Drake famously spotted the Spanish Armada while playing bowls—which is a bit like bocce ball—in Plymouth. Its coast was also the launching point for the *Mayflower*, which set off with about a hundred vagabonds aboard, uncertain what they would find but eager for a new world. The town's historical importance drew regular tourists, yet never managed to capture my imagination as a young boy. (Or as an adult, for that matter.)

———

My family was not worldly by any stretch, but their movements were global. My parents—separately, then as a family—lived all over the world. To be clear, Mum and Dad were not fancy-free vagabonds in their own right. Their travels were bound up in wars and strife; any globe-trotting was driven out of professional responsibilities or duty to their country.

Nevertheless, growing up as a military BRAT (derived from being a British Regiment Attached Traveler) helped cultivate certain vagabond tendencies in me. For one thing, I learned never to presume that I was settled. Until I was eleven years old, we moved every eighteen months, roughly, so mutability felt like a part of my DNA. It seemed that anytime I would start to feel at home, we would receive word that my father—a benevolent navy chaplain—had been stationed elsewhere. It's challenging to create deep or lasting friendships beneath a constant, looming anticipation of departure. For me, it meant that my childhood was a time for harvesting a strong relationship with myself and with the scope and powers of my own imagination.

Fortunately, that left me with a great deal to explore.

I attribute much of my nature to the first decade of my life, and to the lifelong presumption that I would not remain anywhere for long. Lacking a strong sense of place and becoming so reliant on instability was a mixed bag. It prepared me for a life of independence and travel, while likely fostering a risky disregard for consequences, which are more easily ignored—or at least carry less weight—when you don't consider yourself bound to anything, or any one place, or any one person. A fearless mentality can serve you very well as an artist. It also makes it easy to lose control.

Ever since those days, I acutely sense when departure is near, but not with apprehension or dread. Quite the opposite. I long for its pull, forever beleaguered by the question: "Where to next?"

––––––

My maternal grandfather, grandmother, mother, and aunt left the UK and arrived at Ellis Island on a merchant navy ship in the 1920s. Grandpa was described in the ship's manifest as a greaser. I still don't know precisely what that means he did on board—presumably that he worked in the engine room and got his hands dirty.

This is not a coming-to-America story. No dreams were satiated; no bootstrap success or new-world transformation occurred. In fact, my grandmother left shortly after the family arrived. And though my grandfather and the girls remained, I wouldn't say that they ever wholeheartedly immigrated to America, either. The main reason they went was because my two great-aunts had gone ahead of them and done very well for themselves. One of them invited my grandfather to make the journey over and manage a factory. He gave it a few years, but it never amounted to much, and I gather it was quite a struggle for the family, especially since he was raising two daughters on his own. My grandfather was more than happy to return to the life they knew back in England, even though reconciliation with my grandmother was not on the table. After my grandparents' divorce was settled, the girls rarely saw their mother again, apart from an uncomfortable visit here and there.

I adored the rare occasion when I would get to hear my mum speak about her time in America. I would beg her to use that twangy accent, which she was quite good at imitating. She was highly unwilling, for reasons unknown, to indulge my questions about living there. But I knew that they'd practically lived in Harlem, it was so far uptown on the West Side. I suppose that's all they could afford at the time. Despite that reticence, every once in a while, she would surprise me and drop in a sentence, or just a few words, in a thick New York accent, and I would listen, rapt. I thought it was so dramatic and kind of singular that she had that capacity to sound like a different person. Her accent was good enough that, after imitating her, I could vaguely pull off sounding like a New Yorker well before I ever visited the city or dreamed of one day calling it home.

I could also turn it around and occasionally make my mother laugh with my own accents—though after a brief chuckle she would be enraged with me. That was my mother for you. When I was an adolescent boy, I used to tease her by going to the door and pretending to be Mr. Standitch, the local grocer. He was always very flattering: "Mrs. Curry, you are looking very beautiful today. Is it beans that you want?" or whatever. I would creep outside, knock on our door, lower my voice, and announce that I had a delivery. My mother would go to the mirror and make sure she looked as lovely as possible, then open the door with the type of smile I was never privy to. She laughed with surprise the first time she realized I had fooled her—but that laughter quickly transformed into a deep fury that I had raised her hopes, only to disappoint her with my presence.

By the time I was sent on my own to go visit with her father (the greaser), he had been living alone for some time—having separated from my grandmother, who I suspect was not altogether sane. Grandpa was economical with his words and rather sharp-tongued, though not in a mean-spirited way. He called it as he saw it, that's for sure—which I always found amusing. Grandpa came from a long lineage of farmers but had deviated from that tradition to become a seafarer and something of an amateur rugby hero for Devon, Plymouth, and later the navy. He was a scrum half. We had similar physiques, but the comparisons between us ended there—and I was never any good at rugby.

I would have adored for him to be more of a storyteller and did try to get him to share tales of his life at sea and abroad, though he was never anxious to fulfill those requests. He was, however, always prepared to recount his rugby stories, and I listened to those closely. I would even refer back to the cadence of those stories many years later, when I adopted his practically pure Devonshire accent to scrum with the Muppets in my role as Long John Silver.

I almost certainly met my grandmother but was never informed of who she was or that we were even related. An elderly woman lived nearby, and Mum once took me to see her when I was around eight or nine years old. Judy was not included. I had actually seen her around a few times, because she would often be waiting at the bus stop near our home. She only acknowledged me once. Other than that, she would just wait at the bus stop—I presume for a glimpse at her grandchildren.

One day, she stopped Judy and me in the street and said, "Hello. I'm your grandmother."

"You can't be," Judy replied. "Both of our grandmothers are dead." This is what we had been told, after all.

"No, I'm your mother's mother," she insisted. It was quite a surreal moment and my sister and I just stood there, unsure of what to do.

"Here," she muttered, digging through her purse. "Go and buy yourselves an ice cream." She gave us half a crown (which was two shilling and six pence). So we took it, and we did. When we informed our mother afterward, she brushed it off, telling us, "Well, it sounds like that woman wasn't very well, because that's nonsense." But we later learned that my mother checked in on this woman with some regularity, a revelation that, years later, would upset my aunt very much: my grandmother had been cold or absent for most of their lives, and had apparently treated Grandpa very poorly, in addition to leaving him with two young girls to raise.

I learned of my grandmother's death one day in quite a dramatic, Dickensian manner. I was about ten years old, and Mum was out at the shop. A stern older woman knocked on our front door. When I answered it, she looked down at me without a hint of a smile on her lips or a flicker of kindness in her eyes.

"Is your mother home?" she asked flatly.

"No, she's out."

"Well, just tell her that her mother's dead," she instructed, then walked away swiftly.

When Mum returned home, I relayed the message in equally stark terms. She didn't betray any emotion in response, not even a flinch. She simply turned away from me and went to phone her sister, who arrived within a matter of days. At some point during that visit, the two of them went to the flat where my grandmother had apparently lived, which was just a short walk away. Other than the anonymous visit, neither my sister nor I had been offered any knowledge of her existence, let alone proximity.

A note had been left for Mum and my aunt, presumably by the same woman who had knocked on our door to deliver the news to me so abruptly.

"I've taken everything of any value," it read, "because you two don't deserve anything."

She told me about the note a bit later in my life, just as a matter of fact. But she maintained her refusal to acknowledge that it was her mother. Which, to me, demonstrates how far my mother was prepared to detach from the reality of their incredibly strained relationship. How it might have affected Judy or me, as a result, never seemed to factor into her calculation of how much—or how little—she was willing to share.

Chapter Two

The Calm

THROUGHOUT MY MOTHER'S CHILDHOOD, MY GRANDFATHER worked in dockyards and merchant ships all over Europe, including Malta—which is where Mum later met my father, Jim, who was working as a chaplain at the Maltese naval base.

They were a rather odd, highly unlikely pair, my parents. In many ways I find it astonishing that they were the forces that created me, but between my father's empathy and my mother's intensity I can find traces of their influence within the crucial roles I've played and the relationships I've held in my life.

I'm honestly not sure what drew them to each other; such conversations were not shared around the kitchen table, so I can only presume. When they met, my mother was working as a secretary for the British American Tobacco Company along with her sister. Whether out of boredom or intrigue, they started making regular Sunday visits to the Methodist services on base, even though neither of them was remotely religious. Grandpa had nothing against religion, but was certainly never the type of father who would have put his daughters in their Sunday best to take them to church.

My father was not unusually good-looking or wildly charismatic or dynamic, but he was a damn good preacher. He had a definitive style and a clarity in that capacity. There was no doubt about it—he could hold a room. Perhaps Mum was impressed by the way he did that, the way he commanded a service. But he was far more down-to-earth than she was, and perhaps instead it was his simplicity of expression and stability that made him seem like an attractive option for her. For somebody living an uncertain life, he might have been the anchor she craved.

This is all conjecture, of course.

More than anything, I'd wager she was anxious for marriage. And it gave her some kind of stature to be the minister's wife. In time, she learned to play that role convincingly enough (not that she would adapt into becoming pious or a gracious host or anything like that).

In terms of what he saw in her, I can only surmise that my father found my mother stimulating. If you could get a grip on her...well, she was never boring, that's for sure. She had a certain kind of vivacity, really. She could be quite charming if she wanted to be—maybe she was even fun at that time.

They dated briefly, then were married about two years later.

Their wedding was a small, efficient gathering—I don't think her parents even showed up for it. All I really know has been telegraphed to me through the few images I've seen. There's a picture of them outside the church. Dad is in a sharper suit but looks slight and serious, as he does in most photographs. My mother appears to be wearing an enormous, ornate wedding cake on her head. Anecdotally I know that they honeymooned in Bethlehem, which at the time was a bit of a busman's holiday (though it sounds rather on the nose for a minister's holiday, really), and soon after, they left Malta together.

My father was not strikingly handsome; my mother not particularly beautiful. I look more like her, particularly through my eyes. I would have liked to have had his body, which was tall and thin. But my sister Judy got most of those genes.

Photographs reveal my father was an adorable, chubby, happy little boy before growing into the slender young man I knew him to be. His parents, Tom and Gladys, never played a massive role in my life, nor was I ever given ample opportunity to develop a relationship with my aunt Agnes, Dad's sister. But she adored her brother and extended that kindness and care to me when I went to visit her "weeeaaaaayyy up" in the deep northeast of England. I was far from the norm up there, when I went to visit as a public-school boy. But she was great to me, and I loved her for it.

Many years later she would come down to London when I was in *Travesties*, a play by Tom Stoppard. Agnes was fascinated by Soho, and walked through the neighborhood slowly, as though she had woken up in a foreign, unexpected land filled with a sophistication she wasn't sure she could trust. She claimed that she wanted to see me onstage because she was an amateur actress herself, which I had known nothing about and which, given what I knew of her, strikes me as amusing.

I got tickets for my mother and her to see the show. I'm
not sure how much of the play she actually watched, however,
because shortly after taking their seats, Ava Gardner sat down
in front of her. Agnes was beside herself straight on through
dinner, where she continued banging on about it. "Ava Gardner.
Ayva Gahrdner! Ava *blooudy* Gardner. You could've knocked me
down with a feather!" I recall Mother smiling thinly, probably
worried that Agnes's enthusiasm might translate into my feeling
overly pleased with myself.

My father's eldest brother, Uncle Willie, went to Australia
and traveled around on horseback helping to build Methodist
churches. But I never met him until decades on, when I made
a film there. After we wrapped, I got on the plane to Adelaide,
where he lived with my aunt and cousins. He picked me up and
I sat in the car behind him. While we were driving, I scanned
the vast surrounding land where he had made his life, then
turned my gaze forward and was kind of shocked by the back of
his neck: It was just like my father's. The backs of men's necks
in the 1950s and the '60s were usually very short-clipped. I can't
pinpoint why the back of his neck startled me so much. It likely
just came down to a distinct kind of barbering, I suppose. But it
provoked a fleeting moment of longing.

All told, my father was nothing like his amateur actress sister,
nothing like Uncle Willie, and nothing like my mother. He was
remarkably level, with a gentle sense of self even as—perhaps
due to his lineage from miners and builders—he was inclined to
encourage grit and a steel spine. From all the interactions I can
recall, however, he exhibited profound, enduring kindness.

His father was what the Methodist church calls a lay preacher. The congregation is encouraged, if they feel compelled, to get up and preach—even if they're not in the ministry. I guess my grandfather heard that call, and would rise to spread the good word, which in turn is what inspired my father to become a Methodist minister rather than a builder.

Some of my earliest memories bring me back to singing at Dad's church services. It felt like a duty, but one that I was very proud to fulfill, and basically assumed that my little six-year-old voice in the choir was offering people something similar to what my father was providing through an entire sermon.

Judy never joined, though she had a good voice. She would have been mortified to get up there and be scrutinized, as she lacked confidence, whereas I was quite happy standing and entertaining the crowd. And, if I'm being immodest, I probably sounded better than she did.

Singing in the choir usually entailed standing beside a buxom lady sailor and delivering on the high notes. It was a tad precocious and a curious thing to be so young, capturing the attention of a congregation, but I did. And let's be honest: I loved it. The fact that people were offering me attention and admiring my performance was no doubt part of its appeal to me then.

If being praised for my voice made my parents even slightly proud-ish, they never revealed as much to me. That just wasn't the mindset. British parents don't really express pride. Which is a preposterously sweeping diagnosis, I know, so I'll just revise this to say that mine never did. Instead, I perceived from early on that my parents, particularly my mother, disliked it when children put their heads above the parapet. But I don't blame her for that (much). Generally speaking, Brits don't aspire for their kids to be singular in the way American parents seem to— or at least they didn't back then. In fact, they're rather embarrassed if they *are* singled out. And ambition isn't admired in the same way. I don't entirely subscribe to that, nor do I believe that ambition is a vulgar trait, but I've lived in the United States for a while. Point being, there was not a lot of applause or affirmations trumpeting out from the Curry household. Ever.

That's not to say my father was cold or distant; I adored him and eagerly sponged up any lessons he could pass on to me. Perhaps that was partly because I was sent to boarding school when I was ten years old, which is brutally early. But it teaches you to be self-reliant, God knows. Kingswood was a liberal arts school started by John Wesley, who founded Methodism and helped establish the school. That was more of a commercial operation, but they retained a few scholarships for the sons of Methodist ministers, and I received one, which took some of the burden off my mother in terms of schooling and childcare.

The first level was a prep school at Prior's Court, which was a rather grand country house set out by an American army base left over from World War II. I remember at night, I'd often hear the B-52s roaring overhead, wishing I was on one. The school was run by a very eccentric, almost cartoonish Englishman. He was rather smart, if unadventurous, and wholly dedicated to his role. He'd often take groups of boys out to shoot crows on the grounds (they were prevalent in the area), but he'd also take us out to museums and such, hoping to foster in us an interest in art and history and all that. Our headmaster was very merry, very jolly, very judgmental—and married to a mountainous wife. She was a big girl, voluble and steady, and

I think she ran the ship. But in truth, they were as eccentric as each other, and they took our education quite seriously.

Still, when it came to life skills, Dad taught me all the basics, whether it was swimming or riding a bicycle. I was especially excited when I got my bicycle for Christmas, but perhaps not for the reasons young boys are typically jazzed about bicycles. Rather, it was because I had developed a fascination with church architecture, particularly the beautiful Saxon and Norman churches in the west of England. As soon as I could ride, I would set off to find and explore them. My curiosity was boundless and I loved pedaling around Plymouth and into the countryside, wandering as far as my legs could carry me. I never got bored of it.

Though Dad handled the archetypal father-and-son lessons, we connected most profoundly when we used to take walks by the sea. We would talk a bit, mostly about general philosophy, and it was the closest we ever were, I think. Mainly, we just strolled and looked out on the horizon together, which is always positive. Whenever you have the chance, go and find a horizon. It opens up the brain.

My father didn't share much about his personal or internal world. I think both cultural and generational factors influenced his lack of inclination to go into details about his life with me. Even when opportunities presented themselves, he didn't fill in any gaps about his relationships with his parents or siblings, or actively try to impart advice to me. I imagine Judy would have received more of that: both grounded and quiet, they were similar in nature and exceptionally close. They simply adored each other. Judy was Daddy's little girl, and though I longed for a closer relationship with him, I suppose I just accepted it.

Though he never floored me with confessions or much chat, Dad could always make me laugh with his quiet asides and expressive eyes. He often made me the butt of his jokes, but there was a fondness at the root of it all and I never really minded. Once, on a trip to Gibraltar, he wrote me a letter and told me of his adventures up in the mountains. Apparently, he had seen monkeys, or perhaps gibbons, and one of them looked like me. I found it hilarious.

He had a dry sense of humor, but there were few circumstances that he found genuinely amusing—so if he was laughing, we were all laughing. Bless him, he wanted to do good, and he succeeded. It was extremely comforting to be in his gentle and generous presence. He was a legitimately good Christian man, who—despite his vocation—never preached at us or told us what to believe.

Perhaps because he was much more soft-spoken at home, I loved going every week to watch him lead services on whatever base we were living. They never felt like a bore or a chore, because he was never less than interesting. To me, they were my first real taste of performances, and it didn't take me long to want to be involved.

———

When I was eleven years old, Dad had a stroke, which was very sudden. An ambulance came to our home. Unclear of what was happening, I was as concerned as I was confused. I escorted him out to the ambulance, and before being placed into it, he reached for my hand, grasped it, and, with heavy eyes and a sad smile, said, "Take care of your mother."

That was actually a very psychologically damaging thing to say, though of course he didn't intend to be unkind or to burden me with a cruel ask that could never be satiated. He couldn't have realized that he was sending me into a tunnel that had no end. If his stroke was anything like the one I would experience later in life, he did not realize just how dire his health was, and was just referring to the brief period that he believed he would be in hospital.

In any case, I have to trust that he assumed we would see each other again.

He had been planning on driving me back to boarding school that very day; I'd just started Kingswood the year before. The journey without him was long and tedious, particularly as I felt so uncertain about what was going on back at home. While he was in the hospital, Dad contracted pneumonia in serial stages, which was what eventually killed him. Though I would later learn devastating details from my mother, I really had no sense of how sick he was. He was only forty-five. Which is of course awfully young, but at the time, he seemed ancient to me.

Several weeks after arriving at school, the headmaster sent for me and I went to his study, where he gestured for me to sit down. "I have bad news for you," he said quietly. I nodded, wondering what I had done, or why his expression seemed strangely humane.

"I am afraid... it's your father. He is gone."

"Where has he gone?"

"No, no," he paused, rubbing his hands together awkwardly. "He's... well, he is... dead."

I had no way of processing or understanding what that meant, and I was not offered much by way of consolation. I could only nod at whatever words ensued, mumble some sort of thanks, and return to my room. I remained unable to cry, unable to comprehend, unable to grapple with the gravity or finality of what I had just been told. I don't remember precisely what followed, other than being consumed by a feeling that I was terribly alone in the world. Why my mother did not contact me herself or choose to send for me is one of those questions I will never be able to answer. I think she was probably relieved that she did not have to personally deliver the news. She eventually showed up with my aunt Peggy and Judy, whom she had also gotten out of school, and—oddly—took me out for the day to go to Stonehenge.

But before that strange choice of a field trip, my father received a full military funeral, due to his position with the Royal Navy. There was a gun carriage with sailors marching and the whole deal—but neither my sister nor I were allowed to go. I have to assume that Mother thought it would be too much for us, but that wasn't her decision to make, and that angered us both. More than sixty years have passed since that decision, and I have yet to wrap my head around it. Neither of us had the privilege of closure.

After he died, we amassed an impressive stream of letters from sailors across the globe, who wrote to tell us about how Dad had changed their lives, simply by listening and offering good counsel. Though I knew what kind of father he was to me and had a sense of the respect felt by our local parishes about him, those letters showed me what kind of man he was. And if anything was constant or uniform about those sincere messages, it was that Dad had never failed to generously impart his deep-seated empathy to many young men who had been desperately in need of it.

The impression of that tremendous empathy, that profound sense of universal compassion, has had a lasting influence on my life. Fuck knows what those soldiers would have talked to him about when we were living on naval bases. I just know that he listened, he understood, and he brought them solace.

I would never claim that I've ever been able to offer the same selfless service as my father. But that instinct has allowed me to connect with, sympathize with, and hopefully breathe some relatability into extremely bizarre characters, on and off the stage. In large part, I thank my father for that capacity. I consider that stack of letters, all the soldiers who felt seen and heard by him, and who were touched by his compassion. His universal empathy was his greatest gift, and I feel enormously grateful for having inherited some piece of it.

Chapter Three

The Storm

IN THE PERIOD THAT FOLLOWED DAD'S DEATH, THE DISTANCE between my mother and me grew more pronounced. She made it clear that she was not interested in offering or receiving consolation from her children. Instead, she tried to deal with everything almost entirely on her own. Again, I'd love to believe that her intentions were kind: that she didn't want to lay any burden on her children, nor did she want our company for her own grieving process. Yet, while I never witnessed any quiet sobbing, it was clear that she felt victimized by her fate. She had been left as a thirty-nine-year-old widow, in charge of two children. It was a tough row to hoe. She also took her work very seriously, because she knew nobody else was going to step in and provide for us—which I imagine must have been a heavy load to carry.

Soon afterward, Mother's sister Peggy—a name that suited her very well—came down from Coventry to stay with us. She arrived with her husband, a very dashing man named George Guest. He was a bit of a heartbreaker, I suspect, not that I would have had any notion of that as a boy of twelve. The sisters sat by the fire after we had gone to bed, conversing and conspiring about how to handle my mother's situation. I was grateful that they were there, as they were both very kind and helped our mother deal with all the crap that one has to go through following a death: funeral arrangements, dealing with all the admin and costs, getting rid of the clothes.

Awful stuff.

I appreciated that our mother had her sister and wished we could have seen her more often, but I don't think either of them felt the same; it was clear that in times of trouble, they'd show up for one another, but beyond that, they preferred to keep to their own corners. They were sort of antimagnetic, really.

My aunt was a perky number, a real pocket Venus: one of those tiny women with a great figure, an eye for fashion, and enormous flair. Unlike my mother, she was quite flirty and had a lot of natural confidence. I was sent to her one summer for a holiday to bond with my cousin Leslie. I liked her, but she was never really a part of my life. She was a bit demure, really, making it challenging to create an open, authentic relationship. But she was my only cousin in the UK, and we were close in age.

Peggy, on the other hand, was a little bullet, which I found immensely refreshing and charming. The performing arts were not supported by anybody in my family—in fact, I would say they were discouraged by implication—but Aunt Peggy was an exception. She was a leading light in her local drama society. I saw her once in the church hall, performing in a very gloomy piece about women in wartime. Her character, recently widowed, wrote a lot of letters that she recited as she penned them. The letters were not lacking in emotion, and Peggy had a field day. I remember a lot of handkerchief-grasping. She had to break down at one point and was determined to be deeply moving... it was an epic fail, really. But she didn't know that.

Peggy and my mother shared very few qualities other than the huge eyes of my grandfather, which I also inherited. As sisters, they were intensely competitive, and never really seemed to enjoy each other's company. Judy and I went to great lengths to repair that relationship, because we liked Peggy and thought it was sad that Mum didn't have her sister to rely on for any extended period of time. But Peggy rarely made herself emotionally available, unless she was onstage.

My mother had always been a bumpy ride, and not in a fun or eccentric way. She was quite Irish in temperament—I mean midcentury Irish, with a rather harsh, doom-laden view of life. She was raised Catholic, so there was no shortage of drama there. My mother perceived everything, especially anything approaching sin, as being enormously consequential. The slightest transgression—unkindness, even—was given absurd weight. (Though, of course, she was blissfully unaware of her own shortcomings.) She never managed to escape from that cynical perspective, and in many ways, it served as part of our inheritance.

Especially after we lost Dad, she became angry and, when upset, even frightening. Who could blame her? Always lingering just under the surface, her rage was often born of frustration, I think, as she held very high expectations that were often unmet, especially by me. I was quite a relentless child and was no doubt an annoying teenager (as most are), so it took very little to infuriate her. I assume my father had always known that she could be volatile, but that level of behavior had never been on display in his presence. With him gone, though, I was left to more or less fend for myself.

As I grew up, and especially once there were a few thousand miles of distance between us, I came to empathize with her deeply, especially when it came to the raw deal she had received in life. She had been ignored and unloved by her parents. Having had such a strange and distant relationship with her own mother, she had been given no training, no example, of how to be a solid mother herself—so she sort of made it up as she went along. Outside of the family, she also found friendships rather difficult, though she did have a couple of close friends she relied on quite a lot. One woman in particular—an Irish woman— became a very good friend of Mum's, and I became friends with the woman's son, Brian, as well.

Of course, Mum did have the capacity to be loving, in her way. Sometimes overly so. It's just that when she was warm, she was very warm, but when she was cold, she was icy.

I know that it's not attractive to be so truthful about my mother. My memories of her do not deserve a rose tint, but I don't intend to savage her, either. I mention my mother's darker tendencies not because I blame her, nor because I hold these grievances particularly close to the chest. But I can't deny that bearing witness to her rather mercurial character had a lasting impact—of course upon my nature, but more notably upon my work.

Whenever she became irate, my mother's face would change and contort, which scared me, while also making me keenly observant to facial cues and visual expressions of rage. Was I able to play Pennywise—the murderous clown of *It*—or the malevolent, alluring Cardinal Richelieu of *The Three Musketeers* *because* of terrifying childhood memories of my mother? Of course not. Did those memories assist in helping me understand and embody those characters? I believe they did.

And when I was playing Dr. Frank-N-Furter, and emerged from the refrigerator having just murdered Meat Loaf, swinging an ax, was I thinking of her? Well, between us, yes. Yes, perhaps I was.

Nevertheless, I found work that allowed me to process the fear or isolation I felt as a child, and to put it to sleep. Everybody has a well of hurt and darkness somewhere. Many people never find a means to channel it, whereas I've flushed it out often, for a living. People are often terrorized by family members but don't get the opportunity to use that for their own creativity. I, on the other hand, was able to turn moments of having been frightened into being frightening—but in my own way. And my own way was to sprinkle a bit of mischief onto even my most villainous roles, just as I brought a little mischief into my encounters with my mother: doing whatever I could to make the darkness sparkle.

My mother and Peggy had come up as secretaries together, a trade that was useful in the various places all over the world that they'd moved to with Grandpa, and one that my mother would return to after my father's death. My mother was not particularly skilled at deftly navigating all of the unexpected turns life presented to her. Rather than embrace the excitement and unpredictability of that lifestyle, all she ever wanted was to be settled as a respected housewife in a predictable bourgeoise.

A year or two after my father died, she picked up a job as a secretary at the Methodist Education Committee in London, and we moved to Croydon, on the dreary outskirts of the city. There, she decided she could create that regular lifestyle for herself, and essentially modeled her ethos after Margaret Thatcher.

Why Croydon? That's a superb question, as Croydon was one of the dullest places on planet Earth. Somehow, Mum had friends there, and she found work quickly. I wouldn't say she was necessarily happier than she had been in Plymouth, but she enjoyed being that close to London—a place she had always wanted to live. She felt very much like some kind of pioneer for getting those awful commuter trains there and back. A different kind of vagabond, I suppose. She was brave, in her way, but when we made the move, I was about thirteen and my sister was seventeen, so we were grumpier about it than was probably fair.

———

One upside of this rather grim period was that the bond between Judy and me grew stronger, and would stay so for the rest of her life. As to be expected, given the circumstances of our upbringing, we had endured some unpleasant patches earlier in our adolescence. She had left for boarding school when I was probably around seven or eight, so I don't even have particularly vivid memories of this, but she gave me a hard time when we were kids—in part because I always had a slightly easier ride than she did.

Neither Judy nor I were angry by nature, certainly not in the same way as our mum. Judy was four years older than I was, and since she had already been at boarding school for several years once our father died, had to deal with the loss in a very removed way. Like me, she wasn't allowed to attend our father's funeral. That infuriated both of us, but for her, it was a grievance she held for her entire life.

Just as Judy was my father's favorite, I suppose I was my mother's—though I resisted it as much as I could, since it could be overwhelming. Once Mum perceived that I was smart, I became a little dangerous for her because I didn't shy away from the truth, and that wasn't always encouraged. Nothing much was encouraged, really, except for academic success, which there was admittedly little of after I went to boarding school.

Because of all this, I was a bit more resilient than Judy was, and more inclined to talk back to Mum. As a result, when it came to our mother, the arrows came my way. Judy didn't receive the same treatment. She was largely ignored—which in many ways is worse. The difference between how boys and girls are treated was especially pronounced where and when we were growing up. She took a lot of shit from our mother as well, and in time threw some of it back. Whenever she was under attack by our mother's wrath or resentment, I tried to do something about it, to back up my sister, and to be her champion, but I can't say I was especially successful in this endeavor.

I don't blame Judy for being aggressive with me and using me as an outlet for the rage burning within her—after all, that was how our mother had raised us. Fortunately, it didn't last too long. I'm not proud of how I handled this, but after a year of boarding school, I'd learned a few tricks about how to defend myself from bullies, and in a surprising twist, this actually helped my sister and me eventually learn to get along. The first summer I came home, she was being mean to me and started to taunt me about who knows what…but I had been in training for that sort of treatment. So I put her in a headlock and marched her up and down the stairs.

"That's the last time you'll be doing that," I told her.

Again, while I'm not at all proud of the method, it worked. She stopped bullying me and from then on, we became very close, to everybody's great relief. We gave each other courage, and she treated me as an equal and a smart person, which I deeply appreciated.

For much of the time in Croydon, my sister was alone with our mother, who—among other things—thought that the idea of Judy dating, or wanting to date, was somehow hilarious. She didn't think her daughter was very pretty, and she let Judy know as much, which was awful. As to be expected, this had a profound effect on my sister, and Judy went through her whole life, really, without ever realizing that she was indeed beautiful. She particularly hated her curly hair, which was very at odds with the popular British style of the 1960s. I, on the other hand, always found her very striking, and used to urge her to flaunt her extremely curly hair, rather than try to tamp it down and go along with the trends of the day.

———

Meanwhile, I was still finding my own way in the world, far from home at boarding school. The Kingswood campus was nestled in the city of Bath, way up a hill. Like Rome, Bath was built around something like seven hills. We were three-quarters of the way up one of them, in largely horse-breeding country, which was very nice to look at. But the school itself was a little too rigid for my taste, as has been the case with most institutions.

I didn't necessarily share the same hobbies or interests as my classmates, either. Drawn to nature, I used to collect butterflies—and mice, too. I bought them, kept them, fed them some sort of pellets, and then let them go. My little lab for my mice was in a sort of hobby shed at school. I was just interested in putting them together to observe what they did. I was fascinated by them.

Safe to say I was an eccentric, curious kid, which often made me late for less interesting things, like Latin class, which was taught by a man named John Gardner.

"You're late, Curry," he'd say.

"Yes, sir, I'm sorry. I was chasing butterflies," I confessed once.

After that, he called me Butterfly. It was just a means to put me in my place, but it didn't really slow me down. I've always been a bit rambunctious, and I've never held a great deal of respect for authority. My lack of utter obedience would serve me well later in life, but I was much too quick to talk back at that age, to anybody, and was consequently harassed.

Even so, I managed to find allies and advocates, particularly when it came to performing. I loved singing, an interest seeded back to all those naval bases. There was a very cozy piano teacher at Kingswood, Ida Prins-Buttle. (She was originally Ida Buttle, which must have been a cross to bear.) I liked her, and she gave me a lot of attention. She had enough regard for my talent to enter me into ghastly competitions, where I would sing "O for the Wings of a Dove" or something of that dreadful variety.

She took my training rather seriously. When my voice started breaking during puberty, Mrs. Prins-Buttle bothered to contact the Westminster Abbey choirmaster, or the Westminster Abbey Choir School, to ask for a series of appropriate exercises for me so that even though my voice was breaking under the weight of adolescence, it could still emerge as a rather cracked baritone. She believed she had an artist on her hands, which gave me confidence. The vocal exercises she had me do were successful in helping me transition my boyish soprano into a more mature, controlled sound. When I was singing, I was delighted. And while being regarded as either Butterfly or a coddled choirboy was not the ideal way to be noticed by my classmates, bullies were never a match for the fulfillment I felt when I was performing, whether it was singing for an audience or acting on a stage.

Some of my classmates—like my sister did—found it annoying that I accrued extra attention. I wasn't ridiculed excessively for it, I wouldn't say, but I was mocked and viewed as being odd, different. Truth be told, I didn't really give a toss about what they thought—though that may be my perspective today and can be attributed to the luxury of hindsight.

I enjoyed my studies enough, particularly English and French because I was best at them. History fascinated me as well, less because of dates than because of the storytelling. But most significantly, I discovered my love for books. I had a terrific English master, Joe Grieves, who had the whole collection of paperback Penguin Modern Classics with gray-and-white covers. (The orange ones were the earlier Classics.) He encouraged me to borrow all of them, and I did, chewing my way through the whole series, relishing each one. I was happy enough to be in various social settings, but happier when I was reading. I loved to be transported into somebody else's mind. Of course, these interests were early indicators of the vocation I would one day pursue.

When I wasn't reading, I did my best to be sporty. I have always loved being in the water, and can still remember the enormous sense of triumph I felt when I swam a whole length of the pool. At my school I swam competitively for a time, but was far more enamored with the stage. It wasn't even a contest.

John Gardner, the classics master who had called me Butterfly, also directed all of the plays at school—and it was at school where I took the stage for the very first time. Though strict in the classroom, he was very kind to me when it came to acting. I suppose he spotted some talent—or at least a real passion—and was very generous with the roles he gave me to play, roles I remember to this day. There was a play called *Tobias and the Angel*, which had its roots in the biblical canon and follows a young man's journey alongside a disguised archangel named Raphael. I played the young man's father, whose name was Tobit. He was an older man, which for an adolescent boy (I couldn't have been older than thirteen or fourteen at the time) was certainly a stretch, so I felt bolstered by the casting. It signaled that he believed I could do it, which was very affirming to me at that age. We also did *Henry IV* by Pirandello, as well as *The Inspector General*, which was a Russian play. I wasn't the lead, but I had a proper part, despite being one of the youngest actors.

These roles helped me feel more accepted by the theater crew at Kingswood, and I was able to meet some impressive fellow young actors I admired, including a boy named Jonathan Lynn. I remember he starred in our school's production of *Henry IV*—and damn good he was. He was a few years older than me, so we didn't get to act together so much, but in a most fortunate circle back to that time, just a few decades later he wrote and directed me in *Clue*.

In the theater scene, I was also taken up by several teachers who became mentors of a sort. They felt I was gifted, so put in extra time to cultivate my skills. Judy felt that those people paid too much attention to me, and she was right. With time, she was as generous as she could be about the disparity in how we were noticed.

Still, friends my own age were harder to come by. I felt older than my contemporaries, partly because of the loss of my father. I was an easy target for bullies, who used to do things like soak my bed with water, which made for some bitingly cold nights during western England's often frigid winters.

Whenever I could, though, I would strike back with my words. I relish the English language and would defend it to the death. It was (and still is) my best weapon, and I learned to target my vocabulary very specifically at a young age. I had a real knack for reading people, including their sensitivities. That perception would serve me well on the stage and in getting to the heart of characters, but I was perhaps too quick and too able to hit people (verbally) where it hurt them most. There were plenty of bullies at school who weren't impressed by the sharp tongue that I had honed.

Those two factions continued to antagonize and anger me throughout my adolescence, and beyond: authority and bullies.

Chapter Four

Exploring Contradictions

WHILE AT KINGSWOOD, I DID MAKE ONE GREAT FRIEND—who, from the age of fourteen, became a sort of brother to me. Richard Cork and I both excelled as English pupils and shared a robust, like-minded sense of humor, and we both appreciated those qualities in the other. But we were also different enough to benefit from teaching each other new things. Richard taught me so much about art, like how to really look at paintings and how to understand what made for a great one. He always noticed things that I never would, like brushstrokes and how lighting was attained, and his eye for that helped me appreciate visual art in a whole new way. In turn, I suppose I taught Richard a bit about how to not give a shit and stop caring about how the world saw you, though in truth, I think we both gave each other the courage to do that.

I don't think there was ever a period of my life when I took myself *too* seriously, though if there were, it would have been in my adolescence, around the time I met Richard. I likely appeared to have had a great deal of confidence that I didn't feel. I knew how to present well, but I didn't know myself yet.

Ultimately, I've never been a very ordinary person. By my teens, I recognized that in myself and was not always particularly proud of it. I think that was among the reasons Richard and I became such good friends: Neither of us were cut from the same cloth as the rest of our school. If I had to pin down what exactly made us so different, I'd say it was largely about art. We both genuinely appreciated it—be it writing, theater, or painting—and felt kind of separatist because of that. Which sounds quite arrogant, and probably was. But then again, it brought us together, and it was wonderful to have a friend.

That friendship was developed throughout the duration of our time in Kingswood, and continued into our college years, but the apex of it was almost certainly during our gap year in 1964—which is commonly taken in England between secondary school and university, so between eighteen and nineteen years old. We set off in a van for continental Europe and took our time traveling through France, Spain, and eventually into the north of Morocco, specifically Marrakesh and up in the Atlas Mountains, touring the villages and markets.

I loved being by the sea and coast, beside which we often camped. We took up work where we could, doing things like restoring, sanding, and varnishing a docked boat in Cannes. We relished in late nights, enjoying the booze, the people, the food, speaking the language when we were parked in the South of France, and carrying with us the freedom to do and be anything we wanted. At some point, we advertised for somebody to help with money and driving, and picked up a third person, whose name honestly escapes me but who was with us for much of the time. I'm not too sure what he thought of the two of us, but I can't say either of us cared much.

Some of my fondest memories come from our time in Cannes. We were there around the annual film festival and we saw a handful of celebrities going about. We even saw Rex Harrison getting off his yacht and walking down the pier with his wife and a beagle; I'm not sure whether he was there to promote a movie that year or if he might have been on the jury, but it was rather exciting all the same.

Of course, our most meaningful interaction in Cannes happened on an otherwise normal afternoon. We used to walk down to this cheap little bodega for lunch and then pass by the waterfront on our way back to the boat. One day, we spotted Pablo Picasso eating lunch at a café along the route, and Richard practically ran back to the boat to grab his sketchbook so he could start creating his own rendering of Picasso. Noticing our interest, Picasso beckoned us over, turned the page over in Richard's sketchbook, did a silly little sketch of his own on the back, and then signed it. As he handed it to Richard, he smiled and said, "Just in case you want to stay a bit longer in Cannes," meaning that he intended for us to sell it and make a bit of extra cash. (We didn't, of course, although the drawing remains in Richard's book, in his possession.) We were utterly charmed, but I can't say as much for his lunch date: an American woman who was clearly not amused. She looked us over and said, down her nose, "You're *very* lucky that the maestro is talking to you. I hope you understand that." Which, of course, we did.

The adventures I shared with Richard during that gap year were certainly the time in my life when I've felt most free, with perhaps the most relevant and memorable arriving on a night in Marrakesh. Before leaving Spain, we had picked up a bottle of Fundador, which is very cheap brandy, and tastes like it. In case you've avoided the mistake, Fundador is a sweet, almost viscous liquor reminiscent of cough syrup—which didn't keep us from drinking the whole bottle. As soon as we set up camp under a tree in Marrakesh, we passed it back and forth under the stars.

Shortly thereafter, Richard threw up, which must have been an unpleasant relief. I somehow managed to avoid vomiting but my head throbbed and my vision was spinning enough that I had to lie down. But it was in the midst of this liquored haze that we shared one of the most important discussions of my life, talking freely and deeply about just about everything, especially our futures.

That night, we made a pact with each other that continues to serve as a lifelong tenet: henceforth, we would commit ourselves to exploring all our contradictions. We would not tamp them down but would rather see them through to their conclusion. That's a flag that, I believe, I hope, we have both flown ever since.

Exploring your contradictions will mean something different to each person who reads or hears this, but I would recommend such a personal journey to anybody. Nobody knows who the fuck they are, really, for a very long time, and certainly not as a teenager. Sometimes ever. That investigation is a means of getting to know yourself, of assembling your character and accepting that—more often than not—the pieces of yourself may not fit into one box, and that's fine. It's tricky, especially because exploring your contradictions doesn't mean that you're going to resolve them without leaving aspects of yourself behind. But it's worth looking, and invaluable to run those contradictions out to their edges.

That seminal moment, brought on by Fundador, sealed by my pact with Richard, has come to mind in moments of uncertainty throughout my entire life. Because, boy, there were a lot of contradictions for both of us.

For me, exploring my contradictions has meant learning to be comfortable playing a range of parts—personally and professionally—and trying to embrace them all, even if they seem discordant or incompatible. Professionally, the lure of pursuing contradictions has drawn me toward complex characters or compelled me to *make* them more complex and nuanced: so, for example, a scoundrel who is also charming, or somebody rather abhorrent whom I can also play out as being quite irresistible. Those are the roles that have enticed me the most. On a personal level, my exploration has endured and is ongoing.

The whole trip was remarkable. It wasn't just the freedom or the friendship, it was the exposure to the enormous world that was waiting out there for us as we left behind the smaller world we'd come from.

We drove back tan, relaxed, broke—and ready for more. Richard went on to Cambridge, then became the art critic for the prestigious *Evening Standard*, which was a big deal. He deserved it. And as for me? I went my own way. There was never any real falling out or anything; we just drifted apart as our lives became increasingly disparate. I'm not sure what he's doing now, but I hope he's never stopped exploring his own contradictions.

I know I certainly haven't.

Judy never had the same options as I did. She couldn't go from boarding school to a gap year and then on to university. In the 1960s, if you were a middle-class girl in England, you were either going to be a teacher or a nurse. So she went to a teachers' training college, then began working. I went to visit her classroom once she got her first teaching job in Croydon, and there were all these written notices she had placed around the walls for the children, but several of the words were misspelled. Naturally, being a pesky little brother, I didn't hesitate to point out her errors... which she did not appreciate. I'm sure that if she could have written the words "fuck you" in response, she would have.

As soon as Judy found the opportunity, she got the hell out of Dodge and went to work as a teacher for Shell. The oil company had major bases all around the world and provided schooling for their employees' children. She was brave about how she took it in, and they sent her to all sorts of places, like Brunei and Borneo and Qatar. While she was teaching in Qatar, our mother always mispronounced it as "gâteau," which amused us to no end.

In her mid-twenties, she met and married my brother-in-law, who was a big personality in the Shell community. Judy was waiting for someone to really sweep her off her feet, and Stan definitely did that. He was... well, he was more exciting than Croydon—no doubt about that.

He and I never maintained a particularly close relationship—but I tried, as I knew that he made Judy happy, and he was a kind man. We were very different back then; we still are now. He was a supermasculine oil driller, and there was never much of an effort made by either of us, honestly, in terms of creating a meaningful connection. Granted, it can't have been easy for a man on the oil rig to have (the future) Frank-N-Furter for a brother-in-law. But it was still rather unfortunate, because I adored my sister and the children who came along relatively soon after their nuptials.

They eventually moved to a village not far from Norwich. I would regularly go up and spend a couple of weeks with Judy and we would just drive around the county, particularly the seaside towns. We both loved to take in the various villages and the surrounding landscape: it's quite bleak and, in the winter, not at all lush, but that sort of thing was where we'd grown up, so there was a shared element of comfort, of somehow returning to the scenery of our youth.

A lot of lovely memories were made on those drives to places like Woodbridge and Southwold. I particularly enjoyed a town called South Walsham, and Judy used to love to go to Holt, a charming village where we would shop for vintage clothes and antiques. Her two girls picked up a passion for it as well, at least when they were younger.

I have always deeply cherished my nieces and nephew. I've never tired of their company, and I'm still in regular contact with them. They all got Judy's hair, which came from my father (when he still had hair, that is). Of course, they grew up always wanting Twiggy's hair, which was very much in style back then. My niece Kate looks remarkably like Judy to me—at least through her smile and eyes.

Kate and I have always been more alike, especially since we were both quite shy as children. I remember one time, I went to stay with my sis, and young Kate (who was about seven years old) was hiding up in her bedroom. When I went looking for her, I finally found her tucked underneath her dressing table, where she kept all her art studies. She used to spend hours making things out of paper down there. I didn't really have a relationship with her yet, so I told her it was fine for her to stay and hang out there while I sat cross-legged on the floor and chatted with her.

Later on, she told me that she remembered every detail: I was wearing these dark-green-and-brown boots with horizontal stripes that day, which she had never seen before. She called them my "bumblebee boots." Even though I'd only asked how she was doing and tried to have an easy conversation with her, she said that she was mesmerized by my outfit and stunned that an adult was interested in what she was doing and wanted to engage with her. At the time, she told me I was much more interesting than anybody she'd ever met, which I found thrilling and very sweet.

Though it was a simple interaction in many respects, this first moment of real connection was very important to both of us. Our mutual appreciation for art has also remained a cornerstone of our relationship; she's always been very good at art, and I encouraged her to go to art school to refine her talents. I even tried to introduce her to the head of an art school, though I'm not sure they ever met. However, she did end up going to a rather good one in London—and we continue to share our artistic sensibilities to this day.

———

After my gap year, I went up to university in Birmingham to study English and drama. I wasn't as stellar of a student as I could have been, mostly because by then I didn't give a shit about doing anything beyond acting and singing. The academic program was much too rigid for my liking. I almost got thrown out of a final exam, because the overstuffed professor—who did not have a winning personality, it must be said—proclaimed that he had never laid eyes on me before. Thinking back on it now, I do not feel confident enough about the memory to argue that he was wrong. But then again, I didn't have much remorse: I was lazy, I was enjoying myself, and I was exploring.

I had chosen Birmingham primarily because the Shakespeare Institute—a postgraduate research center that opened around 1950 and is a sort of hub for works by and related to the Bard—was attached to it. I learned a great deal at university—not because of instruction per se, but because there were always student plays and productions being put on and I was cast in a huge range of roles. Then and always, I appreciated the wide scope of personalities that I had to take on.

That's the sort of acting career I've always respected most in others: those able to take on all sorts of parts and remain believable in them all. Alec Guinness, for example, is certainly one of my greatest inspirations; one of the things I admire most about him is that he was so completely entrenched into whatever part he was playing. I found him astonishing. I once read that he used to get somebody to watch him walking down the street in his given role, whether it was Colonel Nicholson in *The Bridge on the River Kwai* or George Smiley in the BBC's *Tinker Tailor Soldier Spy*, to see if he would be recognized. Of course, his goal was *not* to be; this exercise helped him measure whether he could get away with blending or disappearing into his character. He did not strive to have a distinct presence as himself, which freed him to assume any character that he wanted to assume. He came out of a different box every time.

I always respected that Guinness was the type of actor who would never be profiled on the front of a glossy, glamorous magazine, because he never wanted to be. I guess I aspired to be that type of an actor, but never really pulled it off. This is likely because, to put myself in place, I also very much wanted to be James Dean. I even recreated one or two famous photographs of Dean with my friend David Fallon. But that's a different, superficial kind of aspiration. That's about image, which I'd like to have cared about less than I have. Within the world of my own characters, I've enjoyed taking a sharp left from whomever I've played before and in whatever venue I've been in before—variety has kept me awake and invigorated. Those without range, who prefer to just play endless variations on one character, should consider just embodying that personality and living it offstage, too.

When I first started acting as a child, I never thought I'd go on to do it as a profession, or perform on a regular basis. There was no question that it brought me great fulfillment, and I never got bored by performing, but I hadn't considered the possibility of "being" an actor and making it my livelihood.

That all changed when I got to university. It was there—I don't remember in which production—that I discovered that I possessed a kind of central, deeply rooted engine that could keep me going onstage. I liked to imagine that it had been built, piece by piece, from childhood, and in spite of pain I endured, like the loss of my father or the challenges I faced with my mother. My confidence as an actor came from that engine and grew stronger, generating a kind of light or radiance from my chest. That beam, I would learn, is also what arrests an audience and holds them—at least from the stage.

Though I was in no shortage of productions at university, I was never officially trained as an actor, even though I studied drama (and English). I was more focused on the academic applications of the field: studying dramatic works, reading plays, learning about the mechanics of being a director or a producer, etc. I didn't trust drama schools; they seemed to turn out uniform products. Students of RADA, the Royal Academy of Dramatic Art, were posh and beautifully spoken, but rather stiff. Those from more method-driven schools like the Drama Centre in London were endlessly writing in notebooks about their characters, to no notable advantage once onstage.

Then and now, I'm slightly baffled to listen to other actors speak fervently about their own process or preparation. I don't have a method to speak of, beyond being mindful about the words on the page and getting into the heart of a character. Not for a lack of being asked, I don't know much about how I act. It's instinctive, and always has been. I've rarely done excessive preparation for my roles.

One hears a lot of pious claims about actors—particularly television or film actors—changing their lives altogether or fully immersing themselves into their characters' beings. That's never been my style. I would never be inclined to, say, adjust how I speak or how I walk, nor would I commit myself to heavy research into a character's relationship with his mother (unless the role was Hamlet).

I don't attempt immersion work, and I have very rarely pursued greater insights than what is presented to me by the writer's hand. Instead, I just read the script—and read it closely. It can be a dangerous practice to go too rogue from the words and direction on the page. It's just not an actor's place to, in my mind.

———

Of course, I hadn't reached such definitive conclusions while I was treading the boards in Birmingham—in part because I was simultaneously throwing myself into the potential of being a musician. During my first year there, I was introduced to soul music and to Billie Holiday, after which I listened to nothing but Billie for probably about a year. I was obsessed with her, with how much she could evoke with her voice in songs like "God Bless the Child" (my personal favorite).

Music had rarely been played in my home growing up. My mother controlled the radio and didn't really want to listen to music or have music as wallpaper; keep in mind that this was the 1950s to '60s, a time when very smart people wrote for British radio. Even so, Mum did get me a record player when I was about fifteen. That was a huge deal (and it made Judy furious). My mother gave it to me around the same time as I landed my first job, as a busboy in a restaurant. I did quite a bit of washing up and getting ordered about, but I didn't mind at all—I was terribly proud that I was making money. It's always nice to get a paycheck. I would use mine to buy a single for my little record player. Louis Armstrong, Benny Goodman, whomever.

Once I got to college, I dabbled in the possibility of becoming a vocalist. On Wednesday nights, I sang with a swing band—I suppose we fancied ourselves to be nostalgia merchants of some sort. We played in any given basement or available room on school grounds. There were five or six of us. We didn't play in front of an audience or anything, even though I would've liked to, of course, being such a terrible show-off. I can't argue that we were particularly melodic or nice on the ear, but we did try hard and essentially just enjoyed ourselves.

I also occasionally stepped in and sang for my landlord, a drunken bandleader who strove for panache (but didn't quite make the mark). He conducted his band in a perennially stained white tux and would have me sing dreadfully cheesy Vegas hits. Still, I leapt at any chance of a gig, especially because he paid me by knocking off a week's worth of rent.

During this time, I'd also often go to Cambridge to visit Richard—he was a member of the renowned Footlights, a rather highbrow sketch group with an impressive alumni list, including John Cleese, Emma Thompson, Peter Cook, Eric Idle, Hugh Laurie, and Stephen Fry. I always enjoyed that.

We also traveled to Italy on holiday for my first time, while we were still in university. Italy struck me as a place where I was invited to be my best person. I remember thinking, "Wow, there's a whole country full of people who behave just as badly as I do...and it's *celebrated*!" The Italians' physical emphasis, their verve, their demonstrative instinct—I loved it all. Italians leave you with absolutely no doubt about how they feel. Alas, that's not the British way, damn it.

Other than such trips, for the most part, my holidays during university were spent working in factories in Birmingham. I had one job where I punched holes in curtain rails. Mind-bending stuff. I felt I shared something resembling camaraderie with the other guys, though I was probably a bit of a mystery to them; they weren't sure what to make of this kid among them. But I always needed to take on extra work, mostly because I had such expensive taste. That came from my mother. Especially once I went to boarding school, she wanted me to look upscale, teaching me that if I looked the part, I could play the role. She also felt going to Kingswood somehow bumped up my social class. Whenever we'd go shopping, she'd make sure to buy me expensive shoes—the type that would make me look like I belonged.

Overall, during my time in Birmingham, I acquired emotional socialism, learned different methods of storytelling and accents, made a few decent friends, and gained a new confidence in myself as a performer (of some sort). But I was far from thrilled to be in university, and by the time I squeaked by and got my degree, I was ready to get the fuck out.

I didn't continue any kind of formal education, dramatic or otherwise. I was twenty-two years old, and felt a strong conviction that wasting another day even pretending to study—rather than journeying out to live in the greater world—would drive me absolutely mad.

Chapter Five

"Blond, Brilliantined, Biblical Hair"

(*Hair*)

I WAS ALL LINED UP TO HAVE A JOB WITH BIRMINGHAM REP as soon as I finished university. Unfortunately (though not really, in the end), I had no agent, and they didn't have a system for trying to get work for young actors, which meant that I didn't have an official contract. Three weeks before I was supposed to start, I was called in and told, unceremoniously, that they weren't going to need me after all.

I was devastated. In retrospect, that was also a damn good introduction to the ever-unreliable world of showbiz. Unsure of what to do next, I went down to London to stay with a friend from college, who was living in Hampstead. As it happened, her sister lived on the ground floor and was married to a successful actor, who kindly introduced me to his agent.

It was 1968, and the provocative rock 'n' roll musical *Hair* had just opened, with an entirely unreliable cast. Several of the actors were hippies who very often wouldn't show up, either because they were too stoned or because they had decided to live in their moment and opted to party instead of work on any given night. I'd seen *Hair* and thought it was amazing, so when this agent mentioned that cast members were being replaced on a fairly regular basis, and suggested that I go for an audition, I was there in a shot. For my audition, I sang my go-to: "Cool" from *West Side Story*. They had a pianist on hand, and I gave him the sheet music and let him know which tempo I wanted to do it in, then began to sing: "*Boy, boy. Crazy boy...*"

The general template for the actors in the production was hippies who could sing, so I was well qualified (though I did have to grow my hair out, so I suppose I wasn't *totally* qualified). Still, I was very nervous, and knew I would have to blague my way onto the show. If I wanted to be an actor, regardless of what was asked of me, I'd have to say, "Yes, I can do that," and then dash off and learn how to fence or ride a horse or whatever was required of me.

So when they asked at my audition if I had forty hours of professional experience and the requisite Equity card (an actor's proof of membership in the trade union), I lied without hesitation. In the spur of the moment, I replied that *of course* I did— I'd done tours of *Cabaret* "in the north." I was called back for two more auditions, and by the time they cast me (and consequently discovered that I was not an Equity member at all), they were happy enough with me to forgo the deceit and even to sponsor my union membership.

And that's how I landed my first acting job out of university, in the original 1968 London production of *Hair*.

That was a colorful experience. But I also treated *Hair* like a drama school. I was initially cast as a member of the troupe, with a role that consisted of jumping up and down among the masses. There was a lot of freedom in the role, which allowed me to experiment with building up my physical presence. And because everyone was kind of vying for attention, I also learned how to make myself *felt* onstage, as a way of distinguishing myself, I suppose. I soon became the understudy to Woof, and eventually ended up playing most of the roles. And yes, of course I got naked. We all did. The performance itself was raucous, as were the nights to follow. During this time, I shared a lovely apartment in Hampstead with about three other fellow members of the cast. It was built on top of a flat roof, and it was mostly made of glass. It felt very modern.

Being in *Hair* offered me not only a ticket to London, but one into a new life, an adult life—made all the more thrilling because our outrageous production was the flavor of the month. We were invited to all sorts of events and, for a fleeting period, we were swanning around restaurants all over town. As a rock musical, *Hair* was an especially ideal gig because it enabled me to stave off a decision I would soon have to make: between music and theater.

When I was still doing *Hair*, I met up with Andrew Lloyd Webber in some horrid little basement in Kensington where he was banging out a few songs from *Jesus Christ Superstar*. There was the possibility I might do the record of it, but it never came to pass. Andrew is an extremely clever man and has also had the very good sense to work with some extraordinary directors and producers. But I don't have a great deal of feeling for his music—I prefer more personal tunes that are of our time and don't strike a derivative tone.

In other words: if I wanted to sing Puccini, I would have gone into opera.

Regardless, it was a thrilling flash of a bulb of time. That type of spotlight is always ephemeral, which is one of the realities I faced directly after *Hair*. I was, at twenty-three years old, suddenly finding myself out of a job, scraping around London for work—after having been given a brief taste of being a part of something that had made a big splash. Before long, I moved to a room in Notting Hill, a neighborhood that is now frightfully grand but was quite a gritty, albeit vibrant, place to be back then. I moved in during a time of widespread civil unrest—in large part due to police harassment of the Black community and consequent uprisings against their mistreatment.

My new digs were a kind of flophouse that was otherwise filled with junkies, and I "shared" a room, which meant there were several mattresses tossed about the floor. Anybody's fate can flip from glamour to despair, but such transitions are practically guaranteed for young actors with little experience and no other resources—like I was. Essentially, I went from working amid a lively cast of a high-profile musical, buzzing to events across town, to literally washing blood off the walls in my apartment before using the restroom. Fortunately, I didn't view it as impossibly grim—I was at that age when you just get on with it. I also continued to revel in my independence, but even so, desperately scrounging for work became rather anxiety-inducing. I was glad that I had been able to secure an agent, who was a nice guy, but he wasn't much use.

All the same, it was an exciting time to be in London: artistically inventive, surrounded by culture, bursting with life. Despite the bloody walls of my bathroom and the uncertainty of my future, I felt lucky to be there, even as I felt like I was out there on my own in the world. The people who ran the companies in which I was interested preferred actors with glamour. I may have inherited my expensive taste and a style of my own, but glamour is something else entirely, and I didn't feel like I had any. Not by my nature, certainly. So I worked quite hard to develop some.

———

In 1969, I briefly worked with the Royal Shakespeare Company—which wasn't nearly as impressive as it sounds. Among the first roles I landed was one as "Hippy" (that was literally my name in the script) in a play called *After Haggerty*. A few of us were meant to represent the Living Theatre, and I remember surging onto the stage at one point. It was useful for my resume, but I couldn't argue that it was a tremendous creative stretch. My illustrious lines were, in totality: "I am not allowed to travel without a passport," and "I'm not allowed to smoke marijuana." There's some irony in that last bit, as there were definitely no restrictions on the amount of dope I was enjoying during that period. After all, this was the late sixties, and there was plenty around.

I'd started smoking spliffs when I first moved to London. I enjoyed the lovely high I would get from mediocre hash. I used to use it in my roast chicken recipe, starting back when I was in

Hair. I'd have people round for dinner, and greet them by asking, "Will you have a glass of wine, or would you rather wait for the stuffing?" On one occasion, my guests were all speaking in a made-up language by the time we got to dessert, they were so smashed. I laughed so hard that I had to hang my head out the window to get fresh air.

———

With acting gigs trickling in so slowly and unpredictably, the idea of being a musician still wasn't off the table for me. But it wasn't a great time for musical artists in England, either. Sounds were being very overproduced, with young singers becoming prey to any number of managers who were grabbing performers and molding their sound into whatever was selling. Ultimately, after *Hair*, I abandoned the pursuit of music and leaned more decidedly into my life as an actor, working at a fated place called the Royal Court Theatre—which I would return to within a few years.

Things were looking up in London and I was having a ball, but I decided it would help develop me as an actor to do a stint working in Glasgow. I was eager to explore a greater range of parts, which I was more likely to get in a repertory company. There were many of these companies across Britain, but Glasgow had a particular reputation for taking on classical plays, and after several years spent playing Woof or Hippy, I was attracted to the idea of exploring more of that classical work.

But I ended up joining the Glasgow Citizens Theatre, which was a very liberal, free-wheeling repertory company run by a man called Giles Havergal. Lindsay Kemp, a director, was also there, and he'd made quite a name for himself as the leader of a troupe of part actors and part mimes. My experience with Lindsay was that, well, outrage was his middle name, really. During my time in *Hair*, the whole theater world had felt like a bit of a whimsical, creative playground. Of course, it's not always this way, and it wasn't the way in which the Citizens Theatre was run.

Though talented and innovative, Lindsay was not someone I felt very safe around. He had no sense of boundaries. He just trampled on everyone—no matter what vegetation was underfoot. Lindsay liked everything to be about himself and was nothing if not self-congratulatory. His vision concluded with a very specific bow that the whole cast had to do at the end of our shows: he told us to imagine that we were on the edge of a skyscraping Woolworths building, then stretch out our arms wide as if to balance ourselves, before bringing them back down again. It was quite showy, but it seemed, to me, to embody who he was.

David Bowie—somebody else whose success would be not just in spite of, but because of being different and challenging norms and gender expectations and all that business—was also, at one point, a member of Lindsay's troupe. During that time, Lindsay and David were especially close. I don't know much about their dynamic, but I do know that Lindsay was the type to bully you as a means of producing results. Having had enough of that throughout my youth, that method never really yielded my best performances.

So I didn't trust Lindsay but I did respect him, because he was so completely who he was. I couldn't even imagine aspiring to that back then. He was very tough with me, particularly when I was playing Solange in Jean Genet's *The Maids*, all dressed up in a corset, a taffeta skirt that I believe was stained with what was meant to look like semen, and tights with holes in them. She was a grubby girl, Solange. As fate would have it—and to my very great fortune—the costume designer, Sue Blane, would later be the designer for *The Rocky Horror Show*. When I was Solange, though, she dressed me in a Victorian corset, worn backward, that she'd found on a cart at a local flea market. I think she paid three pounds for it. She obviously had no idea what it would come to represent, but she was quite ahead of her time.

All of the plays I performed with that troupe, including *The Maids*, convinced me and reinforced my belief that an actor should take risks. Lindsay assisted in cultivating that, but I had to be very careful with him. He resisted doing *anything* by the book. He liked to be able to spin off into fantasy and create his own personality cult. But I recognized the danger in that—and it wasn't the appealing kind of danger.

Still, that taste for creative risk and for the power of shocking or subverting audience expectations has remained with me. From that point on, with few exceptions, I've mainly reveled in taking on parts that have scared me, parts that I initially wasn't sure I could pull off. To nail down a performance piece by piece, *you* must believe it, ensuring the authenticity of your role. If you can do that, no role—no matter how different from your own character it may be—will feel *too* outrageous or *too* challenging or *too* sinister.

Around that time, I also began to appreciate how much an audience responds to a life force. Which sounds obvious, but it's something that can't be generated at will, I don't think. You have to *have* it, this intensity, this magnetism that draws people toward you. I probably recognized that I possessed such a force around that time. I'd always had a lot of extra energy, but I was now learning how to be more intentional about channeling that into my roles onstage, projecting myself with less hesitation and less restraint. Woven into that is the effort to imagine that you carry your own light, and a willingness to project it.

After a year with the Citizens Theatre, and taking on one last role as Buttons in Giles Havergal's version of *Cinderella*, I returned to London and to the Royal Court with a different level of confidence, prepared to embrace risk.

Enough with dreaming it.

I was ready to *be* it.

Chapter Six

"Come Up to the Lab and See What's on the Slab"

(*The Rocky Horror Show*)

THE ROYAL COURT THEATRE WAS (AND STILL IS) A VERY innovative company with a great history of introducing experimental writers, welcoming new ideas, and being loyal to their workers. There were some very bombastic directors there throughout the early years of the 1970s. It was a nest of left-wing shock artists, really.

In 1973, I performed there in a highly forgettable show called *Give the Gaffers Time to Love You*. The director was a super-progressive woman whom I liked very much, as a director and a friend. But the production was...not a triumph. Though

not a grand success, in a curious way it ushered me toward the
role that changed the trajectory of my life.

My role in *Hair* had given me a job and Equity sponsorship,
but it also gave me access to a large crowd of fellow up-and-
coming performers, eccentrics, actors, and creators. Among
them was an actor named Richard O'Brien. He'd been in the
touring cast of *Hair*, so we ran into each other a few times at
parties and knew each other vaguely. Like many of us, I don't
believe he had been particularly bombarded with offers or
opportunities after *Hair*. Fortunately, though, he landed a role
in the London rendition of *Jesus Christ Superstar*, and it was in
this dressing room that he began writing his first play: a sort of
sci-fi musical that incorporated many of his passions. It filled
the time, but also, I believe, was a means for Richard to tap
into his own curiosity about gender and androgyny, which were
slowly emerging in that glam-rock era.

The earliest incarnation of the script was vibrating with sexual impact. There was this intrigue with and interrogation into
fluidity—which, of course, wasn't in the usual parlance then.
Yes, it's a sexual free-for-all, but behind that, it's an interrogation of power—all cloaked in a spoof-like B movie. He initially titled his fledgling work *They Came from Denton High*
(referring to Denton, Texas) and figured it would be great fun
to put it on for a couple of weeks.

Luckily, thanks to his previous roles in *Jesus Christ Superstar* and another smaller musical, Richard was connected to
Jim Sharman, one of the progressive directors at the Royal
Court. Richard told Jim that he was writing a musical that
brought together elements of the zeitgeist that fascinated them
both: rock 'n' roll, B movies, sci-fi, horror flicks, and exuberant

musicals. There wasn't a *ton* there yet, but Jim—a man of exceptional vision—was intrigued by what he read on the page and heard in the songs. Richard Hartley, the music director, was also offered a preview, and liked what he heard. Jim saw promise in the absurd, hokey nature of the original script, which would only amount to an hour onstage. That didn't matter—after all, it's not like they were setting out to create an international cult phenomenon.

Thanks to the support of producer Michael White, who agreed to front the extra cash, Jim brought the show to the Royal Court Theatre for a six-week run upstairs. The upstairs area was generally reserved for risky, risqué, and lower-budget productions, like this one, which was funded by some £2,000 or £2,500. Expectations were set very low—there were only sixty seats upstairs, after all—but the production was green-lit, so Richard set about pulling together a cast and adding some meat to the script.

The plot is based on two newlyweds, Brad and Janet, who stumble into a castle on a quintessentially dark and stormy night. There, they find a carnival of chaos, led by Dr. Frank-N-Furter, a sweet transvestite from Transylvania. After a suitably bizarre introduction, Frank unveils his creation: a well-sculpted, golden-haired man named Rocky. What follows is a wild romp of seduction, betrayal, and intrigue. All innocence is lost, passions are ignited, and the Transylvanians assure that the whole drama is brought to a fittingly surreal and dazzling crescendo.

Richard originally wanted to play the bad boy, a motorcycle-riding character named Eddie, but Jim saw him as Riff Raff, Frank-N-Furter's "trusty handyman." My friend Little Nell (Campbell) is Australian, and Jim discovered her working in front of the theater where *Jesus Christ Superstar* was playing. She used to tap-dance people's ice cream over to them and would entertain the queues waiting to get into the show. Jim admired her dancing skills and charisma, so offered her the part of Columbia. Patricia Quinn, whose lips are so prominently featured, was given the role of Magenta. Marianne Faithfull, who had originally been intended for the part, had fucked off and wasn't available.

Jim Sharman, a fascinating man, was the ideal person for Richard to have found to direct the production. Jim's dad had led a hugely successful traveling sideshow back in Australia. Not a circus, exactly, but an extravaganza of some kind, which he had owned or promoted—so he was notably brilliant at drawing an audience. Having been raised in that kind of setting, it was very challenging for Jim to be bowled over by anybody or anything. He had a taste for the eccentric, and for huge energy. Anything less would bore him. He was also already quite established in the UK at this point. He knew what he was doing.

Perhaps due to growing up surrounded by fantastical spectacles, his method of direction was largely to sit there and try not to be bored. It was his modus operandi: "Come on, wake me up." He had a high, or rather a very low, bar for boredom. I found that challenge very effective, because the last thing I ever wanted to do was bore him. His attitude encouraged me to take chances so that I could grab and hold his, and later the audience's, attention. I was ready to bring that energy to the stage.

Around this time, I was living on Paddington Street, two doors down from a gym and above an Indian restaurant. It smelled like curry all the fucking time. *Spicy.* One fateful night, I was heading into my flat and noticed Richard leaving the gym. He stood out from the rest of the touring cast of *Hair*, which was quite hard to do with that mass of people. We began chatting on the street, and he told me he was in search of a muscleman who could sing. Intrigued, I asked why he needed this muscleman to sing, and he told me that he had written a musical that was going to be performed at the Royal Court.

"You should look into it," he suggested.

Initially, Richard had Jonathan Kramer in mind for the main role. Jonathan had just been in the American production of *Hair* (and would become widely known for the film *Midnight Cowboy*). He was a great guy—smart, funny, and talented. He would have been fantastic. But I was very interested by the small amount O'Brien had told me. Though hardly a muscleman, I went in to see if I might be a fit.

Richard had mentioned that the music would be classic rock 'n' roll, so for the audition, I performed a rendition of Little Richard's "Tutti Frutti." I didn't play the piano, I just came in and said something like "Let's rip it up," then sang and behaved quite badly—sort of throwing myself around the place without a hint of inhibition. I was wearing boots that I had sprayed silver, which I thought were very stylish.

Jim told me nobody else approached the character the way I had. I'd wanted to do something memorable and unique— and it worked. Shortly after my audition, I was cast as a one-of-a-kind modern mad scientist.

His name was Dr. Frank-N-Furter.

———

For everything it's become in the decades since, it should never be forgotten that those are the origins of the show: Richard's concept and composition; Jim's vision and willingness to take a risk; and our being upstairs at the Royal Court, that tiny, gritty theater that only sat sixty people. The intimacy was just what we were going for—it was the ideal way to see and be a part of the play. (As a great many people would later grasp, this show has always been best viewed as a familiar, inclusive experience.) It was also perfect for my character and the skill set I was able to bring to it.

When I accepted the part, I assumed that the character would be a sort of wacky scientist in a lab coat, which is how I initially played Frank in rehearsal. I read for him using a German accent because of the name, and because he was sort of sci-fi villainous, so that tone seemed fitting. By a remarkable chance, again, the marvelous Sue Blane—who knew me from Glasgow—was brought on to handle costume design. She decided to ditch the lab coat and get me back into the corset for the role (the same one would be made to measure and used for the film). When people ask why she picked the corset, I think it's probably because the character was a transvestite and she wanted to blow people's minds, really. And I also had the legs for it.

I bought the shoes myself at a women's shoe shop by finding the most comfortable black heels that came in my size. They did a lot to inform the character, at least for me. When we reunited for the film, Sue adapted them and cleverly stacked them up to create the platforms that I wore. That was less about style and more about helping me keep my balance—but I believe it accomplished both. They were great fun to wear. They've been passed around over the decades, but somehow have made it back to me—and they remain one of the only relics I've kept from any of my work.

Given the minimal budget, I did my own hair for the stage performances, which wasn't a big deal, but I did spend an unbelievable amount of time doing my makeup. I thought Frank's look should have echoes of some of the great villainesses of the screen, like María Casares and Yvonne De Carlo (whom I actually met later on). I also found designer Zandra Rhodes's style quite inspiring; she'd go between bright pink and sometimes slime-green hair, and she was so much fun.

Most of the cosmetics came from Mary Quant; after all, this was 1960s London and the Mary Quant aesthetic was very much en vogue. Eventually, when we went out to LA, I found a lipstick from the line called "Grape" in the Schwab's on Sunset—where I bought all of my makeup—and that became integral to the character. But I always put the most time and attention into my eyes, which—for me—were the most important part.

By the time we made the film, Pierre La Roche, of glitter-rock fame, was brought in to make us look especially fabulous. Pierre was pretty full of himself, but not without good reason; after all, he had just done the cover of a David Bowie album.

One time, as he was doing my makeup, he announced, "And now, we apply the *bleu à la Jagger*."

"Why can't we call it the *bleu à la Curry*?" I asked.

"I don't think so," he replied.

Admittedly, Pierre's interpretation of Frank's makeup was much more high fashion than the sloppy version I'd been slathering on. The decision to implement Pierre's vision actually happened fairly late in rehearsals, but Jim immediately got on board because it elevated Frank and made him that much more absurd—and hopefully more seductive.

Over the years, whenever people have asked me for advice about playing Frank, I've told them the same thing: none of the characters in the show are in drag, not even Frank, and their outfits shouldn't be viewed with such a constrictive lens. We're all wearing what people normally wear in Transylvania. Get the fuck over it. Don't perform like you're dressed in something inappropriate or transgressive; you're wearing the national attire.

(Tangentially, this viewpoint is by no means intended to deride true drag artists, who have been major supporters of *Rocky Horror.* They're a community who gets it and gets on with it. I admire them very much, and plenty of drag artists have dressed up as Dr. Frank-N-Furter. But, again, Frank himself is not wearing drag. In my humble opinion, putting him in that box is one of the biggest mistakes people make when trying to play him.)

Once rehearsals began, the play took on a life of its own. Initially, we didn't care much about what the public's reaction to it would be; we knew we would be performing it in the upstairs venue, the experimental space, and we knew what that meant. Our expectations were tempered accordingly; there would be no skin off anyone's nose if it didn't work. The upside was that there were absolutely no fucking limits, which was very liberating for us as actors. It was also essential to the play's evolution and to our comfort with leaving all inhibitions at the door.

I was faithful to Richard's words and Jim's direction, but within those generous bounds I played with different versions of Frank's character and tried out various personas. What would a 1970s variation of a mad-scientist horror figure sound like? How would he carry himself? We were doing parody, yes, but I wanted to portray Frank as more than just a spoof. I wanted to give a sense of realness to this modern Frankenstein who is obsessed with image and power, even as the role calls for an air of levity (especially when it comes to scenes involving, for example, a cannibalistic feast).

We tried several accents. After we threw out the obnoxious German accent I had originally used, I tried a more universal middle-European vibe... but that felt trite. American wasn't right either—too brash.

At one point, I was sitting on a bus behind an older woman who was talking to her friend. She belonged to a particular social group of women, generally from Knightsbridge, who tended to wear headscarves knotted under the chin. I overheard her ask, *"Do you have a hice in the toewn or a hice in the country?"* Without hesitation, I knew I had found Frank's trademark tone: the woman on the bus, who was doing her very best to sound like the Queen. (It also happened to remind me of the voice my mother used on the telephone whenever she wanted to impress people.)

Though Frank's costume and accent were now established, the discovery of his real nature would develop with time, as I dug deeper into his character. I've been asked an untold number of times about Frank's androgynous sexuality, and how I approached that essential quality of his nature.

A few things are crucial to consider: First, he fucks everybody in the play. The audience has to believe that that is precisely what he wants to do, and that he is entirely liberated to do so. It's a huge challenge but a tremendous opportunity to throw away the barriers of sexual behavior that have been imposed on you. We all exist in a kind of photo-developing bath of sexual contradictions, and the more of them that we recognize, the more fun we can have. In that way, it was a necessary pleasure to explore the nature of desire as I was getting into the role.

Second, actors must remember that their task is to embody the character they're playing. It's not about them, and they need to get out of the way as much as possible, so that Frank's distinct desires can shine through authentically.

And finally, the audience may perceive Frank to be like a woman—but he doesn't behave like one. He is a very strong, aggressive man. He shouldn't camp around.

In other words, if you're going to attempt to truly enter the character, wear your high heels like a man.

———

Staged incorrectly or performed for the wrong audience, *The Rocky Horror Show* would have been a far too outrageous pill to swallow. We would not have lasted the week at one of London's more established venues. Happily, the Royal Court wasn't known for having a conservative audience.

Gloria Taylor, the publicist, had the ingenious idea of inviting some smart, funny people to be in the audience (like Rudolf Nureyev, who became a great friend). She used to bring her six-year-old son, Sid, to rehearsals. He'd sit with his legs crossed, enjoying the spectacle. As it happens, he's an actor now, Alexander Siddig, and part of the Sudanese royal family. Anyhow, her idea of having those clever people in the audience helped contribute to a spectacular launch, and so our "strange journey" began, on June 19, 1973.

The opening of *The Rocky Horror Show* was among the most magical experiences I've been privileged enough to witness.

There happened to be lots of thunder and lightning that night, which was a wonderful and very cosmically generous addition to the show.

From the first moment, the production was greeted with more joy and appreciation than we could have imagined. The audience *got it*. They were immediately a part of the zany, surreal, nostalgic experience. That was the real magic, and it felt supernatural, as none of us were certain if the viewers were going to get it at all—it seemed equally likely that they would just walk out.

Standing onstage as we gave our first bow to an enthusiastic crowd, I knew we'd pulled it off. I remember having a distinct feeling that I was drawing energy up through the boards, through my high heels, and into my body. There's nothing like that feeling, that surge of energy that allows me to manifest my character completely. Such a phenomenon comes more naturally on the stage, though in time, I found a way of engaging with the camera to feed off it similarly. Manipulating a camera requires more focus and intention, as opposed to the organic rush of energy the audience feeds you when you're onstage.

Regardless, I felt like my light had been illuminated. I was beaming. My engine was running.

The extraordinary rush from our first performance seemed to be shared with the rest of the cast. We were all high off it. As a production, there was a sense that we'd done something unusual, something that would raise eyebrows, something that would make people uncomfortable but that also might have the power to make people feel *more* comfortable about being unusual. That was a magical sensation.

It still is.

In a few blinks of an eye, the show became a huge hit. It was suddenly the trendy, edgy, unexpected performance that people were talking about.

The first of the Royals to come see it was Princess Margaret. There was a bomb threat the night she was there, so there was a huge crowd of people who had been evacuated out on the sidewalk. She was a bit scared, as one would be. When somebody asked her what she thought of the show, she relaxed a little. "Funny... I truly enjoyed it," she said.

A princess's approval certainly didn't hurt.

David Bowie was also amid those early audiences, and came a few times, always bringing a whole entourage along with him. He made a big show of ostentatiously clapping over his head whenever I came on. Bowie and I ended up having dinner several times while the show was running there, at a hip joint across the street called the Casserole. Most dinners were by accident: we would both show up around the same time and join tables. He was good to me and never pulled rank—which he could have, because he was massive at the time.

His wife Angie was a character. Some may disagree with me, but she was the first person whom I remember shouting loudly enough to be considered audience participation. When Riff Raff was trying to kill me, for example, she yelled out a warning—"No, don't do it!"—in what seemed to be genuine, instinctive protest.

Before long, I began being recognized on the street, with the press comparing me to the likes of Bowie and also Mick Jagger—presumably because of Frank's androgynous looks and very open, blatant sexuality. I grew to be friendly enough with them both, though we're all very different. Mick was, around that time, trying to project himself as a kind of shaman. Bowie just wanted to be a modern artist. I think he would have been very happy to just paint.

Though I met a lot of very interesting people during these early shows, one of my favorites was a fabulous woman I met at the Casserole. During my time as Frank, I was at that restaurant most nights, since whenever you're doing a show, you're always starving at the end of it. A good food source is invaluable.

Anyways, quite early on in the run, I met this woman named Amanda Lear, an incredibly stylish blonde with this growly voice. I was absolutely fascinated by her. She was as brilliant in conversation as she was in looks, and her looks were brilliant. She was gorgeous in a completely 1970s sort of way. Her hair was always windblown, like she had her own fan. The first time she saw me, she beelined across the restaurant and plonked herself down at my table, right across from me.

"I *have* to meet you," she told me, "because we are important, the two of us."

She was drawn to the allure of the show, and anytime we found ourselves in that restaurant around the same time, she'd seek me out. It must've been exhausting to present herself with as much energy and vivacity as she did, but she was always totally present and unapologetic—a real star in her own right. Roxy Music star Bryan Ferry picked up on her very quickly (I think the two were briefly engaged at one point) and even put her on the cover of *For Your Pleasure*, their 1973 rock album. Later, in the 1980s, she moved to Paris and became a sort of disco sensation, growling to 125 bpm.

Frank may have commanded the stage, but Amanda certainly dominated the world outside of it. She'd always say, "Why the fuck not, darling? You can't have all the fun. You're not even real!"

———

When fame came my way, or at least enough notoriety that my mother's friends were sending her publicity clips of the show, my mother took the solid stance of: "Who do you think you are?" However lucky I've been about channeling my mother's palpable anger, that seed of self-doubt—planted amid my greatest triumph up to that point—still remains. She had raised me to distrust applause and praise, making it difficult for me to ever fully accept any accolades received.

Judy and I weren't speaking a ton at the time, because I was so involved in the play and she was just falling in love and starting a family. Still, she was truly happy for me when I became successful, and the sole person I could depend upon to love whatever I was doing—no matter how outlandish. People who are authentically happy for you are hard to find, and I felt lucky to count my own sister among one of my own.

Before long, *The Rocky Horror Show* gained enough attention that we had to leave the Royal Court. We were offered West End theaters, but they didn't feel quite right. Jim and our producers managed to find a cinema, the Chelsea Classic, which was going to be pulled down in three months. That meant the rent was reasonable, which in turn meant that we didn't have to charge too much for the tickets. We stayed there for the cinema's last three months, and the upgrade allowed us to get accustomed to performing in front of a more expansive audience while still maintaining that intimate feel. When they demolished the theater, we moved on down to the larger—yet still suitably dodgy—cinema Kings Road. If memory serves, we may have even opened there on Halloween, which was never as big of a deal in England back then as it was in America. And that's a shame. (Though I suppose the popularity of the holiday has grown a bit in England over the years.)

Kings Road is where Lou Adler, a well-heeled American film and record producer, first saw the show, after being encouraged to do so by Britt Ekland (an actress, his then-girlfriend, and the mother of his son). She told him it was the "in" cultural event in London. Evidently, Lou took to it. He appreciated its potential and noted the buzzy response the show was receiving. The day after he saw the production, he bought US touring rights from Richard, and six months later, we were off to Los Angeles.

American Equity made it very difficult and expensive to take entire English companies to America and vice versa, so I was the only member of the original cast who was allowed to go. Jim came, too, of course. We were with an American company there for nearly seven months, which is when Meat Loaf joined the production.

In LA, we performed at a swanky place on the Sunset Strip called the Roxy. The theater had originally been a strip club called the Largo, built in the Philip Marlowe–esque 1940s. It had been taken over in the early seventies by a group of rock 'n' roll nobles (including Lou) who wanted to make it into a kind of showcase club (which it later became). They had been looking for something closer to a type of cabaret, and when Lou saw *The Rocky Horror Show* in London, he decided it would be perfect for the venue.

Our LA production premiered in March 1974 and—just
as it had been back in England—the show was an instant hit.
Opening night was something to behold; Lou had a searchlight
that was beaming across the night sky, and big names like Mick
and Bianca Jagger, Jack Nicholson, Roman Polanski, and John
Lennon all showed up.

Lou also invited Gordon Stulberg of Fox to come see the
play. He connected with its zaniness, and in about as much time
as it had taken for Lou to buy the US rights from Richard, Fox
made a deal to turn the show into a low-budget movie.

———

Few things are ever the way you expect them to be, as was the
case with my first time visiting the United States. The pace there
was slower than in London, by my impression, but Hollywood
was sufficiently tacky around the edges. Beyond expectations,
the experience freed me an awful lot. Nobody had a clue or gave
a shit who I was. I was liberated to completely reinvent myself
if I wanted to, personally or professionally. It was eye-opening
and highly valuable to witness firsthand what was expected of
theater actors in the States. In the 1970s, British musical actors
didn't have to have boundless energy. Not like they did on Broadway. (That standard has changed over the years, and UK actors
have learned how to attack performances with a similar kind of
exuberance required for a musical, but back then, it wasn't the
same.) Though my role as Frank didn't change dramatically once
I landed in LA, my performance became much more intense—
partly, I'm sure, because I was determined to make an impression.
Ultimately, meeting the amped-up standards of American acting
became invaluable for the entirety of my career.

For the first few months that I was there performing *Rocky Horror*, I stayed at the Chateau Marmont. It wasn't exactly the kind of place that provided you with breakfast, but they would bring you a pot of coffee. My apartment had a kitchen and a dining room, which I loved. I remember there was a guy behind the desk, a leather motorcycle queen, who always used to answer the phone, "Chateau Marrrrr-mont?" like it was some kind of orgy den. It was a colorful place, to be sure.

Later on, I stayed with my then-manager, Barry Krost (who also managed Cat Stevens, among others), and then moved over to a very smart, highly bizarre building called Sunset Tower (which briefly became the St. James's Club hotel). It was fabulous-looking, sort of classic Streamline Moderne. And it was an exciting time to be there: Stacy Keach lived next door to me and Diana Ross had her office in the penthouse. I used to see her in the lobby, beneath piles of shopping from Beverly Hills. "Could you please press the button for the elevator for me?" she'd ask, waiting until someone came over to assist her. I had a feeling it was because she had fabulous long fingernails, the type of talons rivaled only by Barbra Streisand. I was delighted to oblige.

Iggy Pop lived there as well, which meant that the ambulance would arrive at least once a month, because—as legend went—among Iggy's party tricks was to dive from his seventh-floor apartment into the pool below. Occasionally, he even landed in it.

In other words, drugs had arrived in Los Angeles.

Socially, I found the party scene much heavier in LA than in London. In my early days there, I didn't do coke yet and didn't smoke that much dope anymore. It wasn't good for my voice, plus I had sort of smoked my fill when I was in *Hair*. I was well acquainted with that variety of mind expansion, had enjoyed it well enough, yet felt I was over it. Don't get me wrong, I wasn't deep into clean living and hikes through the Hollywood hills— I still drank far too much. Across the board; across the globe. When I start, I usually have a very hard time putting my foot on the brake. One leads to two extremely easily. And then to seven or eight.

All that aside, it was a fantastic time of my life to be introduced to Los Angeles. Lou was very good to me and made sure that I felt welcome there. Mick had seen the show in London, but the first time I met him properly was when we all went for lunch at Lou's place in Malibu, early in my LA tenure. Mick and his wife Bianca were traveling through on a sort of royal tour.

I had largely been introduced to rock 'n' roll by the Rolling Stones—they were already very well established by this point, with more than a handful of number-one hits to their name. When they came out to Lou's for the afternoon, that was a real moment (for me). I was very shy with Mick, but he was pleasant with me. Bianca was always a piece of work. She had brought along a bag with ten different suntan lotions, which she proceeded to pull out one by one to show me. "Thees one is perfect for the South of France, thees one is very good for Bra-*zeel*, ahh, and here is the one for LA," she explained, though I couldn't have been less interested. We didn't interact much after that. She did not appeal. But Mick wasn't embarrassed by her, not at all.

After lunch, they gave me a ride to the theater in their limo, because I didn't have a ride to work and didn't drive at the time.

Tim's mum and dad on their wedding day before leaving for their honeymoon. *Photo courtesy of Tim Curry's personal collection*

The most beautiful baby in Hong Kong, 1947. *Photo courtesy of Tim Curry's personal collection*

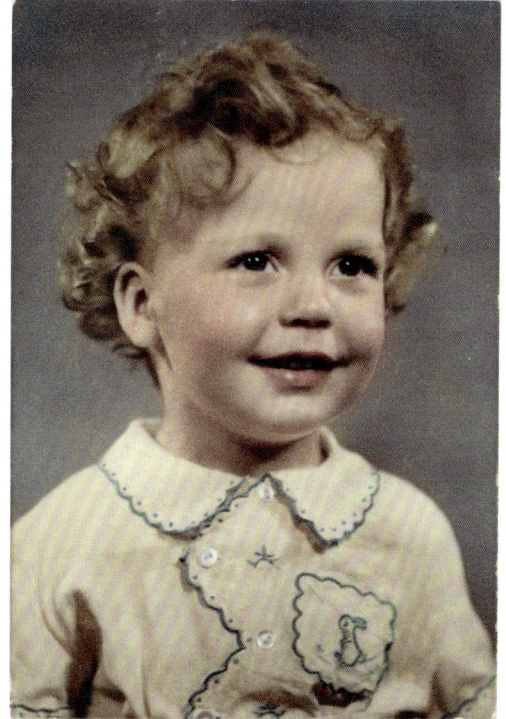

Tim and his sister, Judy, 1947. *Photo courtesy of Tim Curry's personal collection*

Tim with his dad, Judy, and Grandma Curry. *Photo courtesy of Tim Curry's personal collection*

Tim with his mum, Judy, and Granddad, Langmeade. *Photo courtesy of Tim Curry's personal collection*

Tim with his dad and sister, Judy. *Photo courtesy of Tim Curry's personal collection*

Grandmother Curry in front of her sweet shop. *Photo courtesy of Tim Curry's personal collection*

Tim with his mum in London, 1968. *Photo courtesy of Tim Curry's personal collection*

Tim's first professional headshot taken by John Vere Brown, which appeared in the programme for the musical *Hair*, 1968. *Photo courtesy of Mander and Mitchenson / University of Bristol / ArenaPAL*

Tim doing his own hair and makeup backstage during *The Rocky Horror Show* at the Kings Road Theatre, 1974. *Photo courtesy of Joe Gaffney*

Tim and Meat Loaf chatting outside the Belasco Theatre stage door on Broadway after a performance of *The Rocky Horror Show*, 1975. *Photo courtesy of Sunny Bak*

Tim, Peter Hinwood, Susan Sarandon, Nell Campbell, and Barry Bostwick after filming the pool scene in *The Rocky Horror Picture Show*, 1975. *Photo courtesy of Estate of Mick Rock 2025*

Stephen Moore, Tim, and Michael Palin in *Three Men in a Boat*, 1975. *Photo courtesy of BBC Archive*

Poster advertising two of Tim's live appearances during the *Fearless* tour, August 1979. *Photo courtesy of Lou Adler*

They also came to see the show again that evening. Bianca was wearing a white toga with a large garland of flowers around her head. I was hiding in the box office on the street, because I used to make my entrance as Dr. Frank-N-Furter from the back of the theater onto a ramp that went right down through the middle of the audience. While nestled there, I heard them walk in, amid a flurry of flashbulbs and paparazzi.

"Meeck," she said, "we cannot keep going out all the time like this."

"Yeah, yeah, roooiight, Bianca," he roared with laughter.

It was clear neither of them hated the attention.

I eventually developed a lovely friendship with the Jaggers, especially Bianca. Years later, she even invited me to her birthday party at Studio 54—the one where the photographers got that infamous shot of her up on a white horse.

Say what you will, the woman always knew how to make an entrance.

———

I tended to get a little more nervous for shows in the States, depending on where we were in the run and who was in the house. As the show got bigger and bigger, more and more stars came out to see it. Keith Moon, the drummer from the Who, was often there, and Carole King arrived dressed up as Magenta, I believe. Jack Nicholson came, too; he was a great friend of Lou's and very kind to me. One time, Nicholson even took me to a Lakers basketball game, where he had seats on the floor. That was wild—a very different experience for me to be in the middle of *that* kind of blaze. We chatted amicably through the game, and though I was no basketball fanatic, I appreciated

the gesture very much, as he was a rather huge star at the time
(still is), and he didn't need to extend the invitation.

After those whirlwind six or seven months at the Roxy, Jim,
Lou, and I went back to England to shoot the film. Meat Loaf
came along as well. After we were done filming, which was
exhausting, the play finally made its way to Broadway, to play at
the storied Belasco, which had also been remodeled into a cabaret theater. It was March of 1975.

It would be quite an understatement to state that we did not
make it in New York.

The Rocky Horror Show was a spectacular failure on Broadway; I mean the truest of flops. Clive Barnes from *The New York
Times* had loved it in London and LA, but I suppose his standards for Broadway were measured differently. Or perhaps the
show was a bit after its time by then? The Theatre of the Ridiculous had already been a big hit, and maybe New York didn't have
any more appetite for a pop-art, gender-bending spoof musical,
or for what Barnes referred to as another "British invasion of
Broadway." Maybe the interruption of the film had interrupted
the flow. Maybe the hype was too overwhelming.

Whatever the reason for the negativity, it was my great mis-
fortune to learn about the reviews in real time, live on *The Today
Show*, the morning following our opening night party. I was
rather bleary-eyed and had to sit there listening to them read
aloud the critical response, which was unkind at best. We then
had to chat about what a shocking letdown the show had been.
It was fiendish of them to do that, and a horrendous way to
learn of the public's reaction.

With a bit of bile in my mouth, I can confirm any rumors
about how one gets treated in New York following such negative

reviews. People would spot me, then make a point of crossing the street in avoidance. It was as though being poorly received by Broadway critics turns one into an actual pariah.

Before long, we were playing to dozens of baffled nurses who had received free tickets to a Broadway show. It was very strange.

In all, the show only ran about forty times until we were shut down. I try to curb my memories about that dreadful reception, and my consequent devastation, by remembering the kindness and generosity of the manager at the Algonquin, the lovely hotel where I was staying for the duration of the play. It was (and is) luxurious. I discovered just how luxurious when the play closed abruptly and I was left unable to afford my bill.

With no small amount of mortification, I had to approach the manager of the hotel and inform him of my situation. "I... well, sir, the thing is ... they closed the play prematurely and... well, I'm unable to pay the bill," I admitted, my head bowed, face flushed.

Without missing a beat, he said gracefully, "Well, you'll be back. Pay me when you can." I was so relieved I don't think I was able to summon up any words.

So it felt tremendously gratifying when, within a matter of months, I was able to return with *Travesties*, which was a huge hit. I was filled with excitement as I walked briskly into the Algonquin and counted out exactly what I owed him, paying off my debt with a large stack of five-dollar bills.

He smiled benevolently and nodded his head. "I knew you'd be back."

Chapter Seven

"Let's Do the Time Warp Again"

(*The Rocky Horror Picture Show*)

B ACK WHEN WE WERE STILL PERFORMING IN LONDON AND the show was getting all the hype, the idea of a movie had started to take shape. Several big-name personalities threw their caps in to play Frank onscreen, with the likes of Mick Jagger and several other celebrities expressing interest in filling the role. But Jim Sharman, who directed both the play and the film, wasn't dazzled by them at all.

Jim and Richard O'Brien, bless them, were very faithful to me. As was Lou Adler, who had brought the play stateside and cut the deal with 20th Century Fox, and would be coproducing the film. Jim made it clear to me that he was not seriously considering anybody else. And this may be hubris, but I honestly don't think that Lou had any interest in being involved unless I stayed on as Frank.

Many people believed (and felt compelled to tell me) that popping my cinematic cherry by playing such a uniquely extreme character would be damaging to any future hopes I might have for a film career—or at least any career that didn't cast me as a power-hungry omnisexual transvestite in fishnets. Their instincts may have been right, but I felt they were wrong, and I certainly wasn't about to take a step back and watch somebody else play the character. By my memory, that was the most frequent question I fielded, especially in my earlier career: Was I afraid that I would be forever typecast by the decision to play Dr. Frank-N-Furter? Would I ever be able to escape from Transylvania? People were still asking me those questions when I would be coming offstage from finishing a rock concert with my band, while I was still in my costume wearing Mozart's frock, while I was literally coated with plaster as the embodiment of evil, or just after performing a dance routine for *Me and My Girl*.

I understand where the question comes from, of course. Frank is an indelible, unforgettable, one-of-a-kind character. It's easy to see why people might assume he'd be inescapable. But I got so *annoyed* with the question. Thankfully, I never found that to be the case and was able to break out of that mold (though it's not like there are many characters I've come across in the years since that are anything like Frank).

The last thing I'm attempting to do is disparage how lucky I was to have played him for all those years. Playing somebody like that wakes you up to new dimensions of human nature. I can't imagine a better role to enable me to embrace my contradictions and see them through. I learned not to limit myself—artistically, professionally, sexually, or mentally. Over the course of thousands of appearances, on and off the stage, stepping into Frank's very high-heeled shoes forced me to carry a persona of real confidence. It had to be very convincing. That didn't come naturally to me—I've always been overly self-critical, and I came from a family that never hesitated to point out my shortcomings—but in time, it got easier. Being an actor, particularly a routine bad guy in such an experimental work, required me to shed as much of that baggage as I could so that I could just get on with it.

Having been in America in the interim—between staging it in London and returning to create the film—was of great assistance in helping with the presence that the filming would require. By the time we started production I had a stronger handle on how to draw that up. Frank had to command the room *and* take on the camera. It wasn't like Jim directed me, "Tim, break the fourth wall" or anything like that. It was what it was: a natural means of taking control over everybody in the room, including those filming. But in staying true to the character, I was able to convey his brilliance across either medium.

Any grievance I have held is not with the character nor with any of those directly involved. But as we ramped up to the filming, and of course afterward, I grew exhausted with all of the publicity. I have a natural aversion to it, though I'm aware that it's part of the game that needs to be played.

From the earliest days of my career, I've always been repelled by the idea of self-promotion. I'm sure the "Who do you think you are?" refrain in my mind plays some role in all that. But I still don't love to talk about myself (he states *while penning a memoir...*), and I found it especially problematic in my early twenties because I didn't have a firm grasp on who I was yet. And movie publicity is far more demanding about interrogating all those "behind the scenes" details. I knew I had to take a stab at it, though I proceeded with caution.

I don't admire the part of show business that deems your personal life public property. I mean, it's all very well when you're happy, but it can be extremely nasty when you're not. And I frankly don't think it's anybody's business. I disagree with anybody who believes that you are depriving people from enjoying a production if you don't bare your soul to the public while you're taking on a role.

I usually tried to keep it down to one or two big interviews per year, often when I wanted to try to help sell something. After all, I do understand that it has become part of the whole deal, and that you really have to get on with it. Still, I find it intrusive. The biggest drawback is if people become really rabid fans, then learn about you and suddenly think they've bonded with you or—in the worst extremes—that they sort of own you. Then you have to disabuse them of the fact, by saying something like, "I'm just a person, and I'm not *your* person." Which is rude, I suppose, but has proven necessary on occasion.

People have either been offended or intrigued by my reticence. I understand in retrospect why it might pique curiosity. People saw a dissonance because I played the type of character (the force that is Dr. Frank-N-Furter) who would have been abundantly comfortable giving interviews and being in the spotlight, but then I would emerge from backstage with no interest in talking to... anyone.

Publicity avoidance was also motivated by my experience of interviewers coming to me with some sort of agenda. I would have to shake off all the inevitable coverage that's simply untrue, as it so often is. I've found that whenever you try to bring a nuanced, balanced answer to something, the interviewers always want something more from you. And if you don't bring them something more, something that hasn't been said before, they lose interest. And why not? But it can be rather difficult at times, because you have to introduce some elements of surprise in order not to totally bore their pants off. (Though *that* would be fun.)

I envy those for whom being interviewed comes so naturally, and who don't have to waste time eyeing reporters and maneuvering around them. A lot of stars really love the whole deal. Some even seem to love the publicity more than the acting.

I see that comfort with publicity with younger generations that might feel more comfortable with such attention—but I suppose they've grown up on phones and cameras, already in a world that marries the public and the personal, where people practice their answers and construct a personality that feels unique. Maybe it's not generational. Bowie and Mick never shied away from an interview. We're roughly the same age, and they also grew up as suburban British boys like me. So I guess it's not quite as simple. Some people are made for it and others avoid it at all costs.

Whatever way you want to look at it, *Rocky Horror* made public scrutiny inevitable—especially after the phenomenon of the midnight movie hit in April of 1976, seven months after the film had come out. The assumptions made about me ran (and perhaps continue to run) the gamut. People often expected me to be brash or aggressive, like Frank. That's still what is most desired from me when I meet strangers. I know I've disappointed audiences because I'm much quieter and more reserved. (Though I don't really know anybody who's less reserved than that character... I'm not sure such a person could get on in everyday society.) If I actually existed on Frank's level in my everyday life, I would have burnt out long ago.

Singular as his character is, I never found it hard to connect or empathize with Frank. He is enormously sexually driven. That's vital to who he is, but it's also sort of tough on him. He's kind of up to his neck in hormone soup. "Give yourself over to absolute pleasure. Swim the warm waters of sins of the flesh." That's not as luxurious as it sounds; it's actually part of what eventually makes him so vulnerable. It's also a physically exhausting philosophy, and one I pretty much took to heart at the time.

The toughest bit for me, in playing Frank for all those years, was becoming somebody so consciously aggressive and manipulative. It was particularly tricky to embody that in a musical. Musicals are all about joy. I think most people come to them, in fact, to tune out reality and just mainline joy. Reconciling that with some of Frank's less admirable behavior was complex.

Ultimately, though, playing such an unusual character taught me a great deal about myself, as an actor and as a person. One thing I discovered was how difficult it is for me to cry, first onstage then later while the cameras were rolling. I can do it, of course. But it's hard. I don't think of anything specific. When I'm working, genuine emotion comes from somewhere very central to me, almost from my gut. I've had enough things in my past that could make me start sobbing—but I don't tap into them intentionally while performing. That would get in the way—or be very disruptive—in terms of authentically embodying a character. Because to do so would require leaving the moment.

It's not at all hard to laugh while acting—and it's something I've done in every role I've played. I can always find the humor and have rarely played a character entirely devoid of it. The laughter is authentic, though of course I adjust it to the manner in which my character would laugh.

People also expected me to be something of a sex symbol, given the nature of Frank's extremely open relationship with... EVERYBODY. I was aware of the reputation, but it always felt like a label better avoided. It's a dangerous trap. Professionally, it's limiting, since it can limit the way that directors see you (though, if they're honest, most of them like it just as much as the audience does).

Personally, it was perhaps even more challenging, as I never knew what about me people were drawn toward. At times, I've found it pretty painful. It's incredibly uncomfortable for strangers to just come up and tell you that they fantasize about you. And it can make your own sexual responses dangerous because you don't really know why people are talking to you. You know perfectly well that you're as dull and boring as everybody else is.

Naturally, it's fun to play somebody who is later perceived as some sort of ambassador for unleashing other people's self-discovery and sexual liberation. I love the notion that Frank has helped release people's inner freaks or given them permission and passports to emerge and be celebrated. I've been told as much many times, and I hope that that legacy continues.

It's an odd pairing: I've always loved an audience, just from a distance. Once you've elicited a strong response from an audience, you want it again. And again. That kind of energy is as addictive as any narcotic. It's terribly easy to reach a state of only feeling truly alive, or your most alive, in that capacity. Many performance artists reach that level. But you have to be careful: it will always desert you, sooner or later. Audiences dry up, of course. And it will feel at best strange, and at worst unbearable, when you cannot summon that high any longer.

———

Even though I played Frank in both adaptations, the play and the movie were wildly different experiences, especially as I had never been in a film before. The play had been staged in an intimate, abandoned cinema (where Dr. Frank-N-Furter works and lives), rather than a massive spooky manor. They decided to film in a decrepit castle called Oakley Court, located in Windsor, just outside of London. It was sort of Victorian Gothic, built in the late nineteenth century, which seemed perfect for Frank-N-Furter's lab and mansion. But it was falling apart, intentionally, as it had been in disrepair for so long and the owners wanted to renovate it into a swanky hotel (which they have since done, I believe). It was not exactly the epitome of luxury, nor should it have been. Notably, the place didn't have heat or bathrooms. I think the whole building had been scheduled for demolition before we even stepped foot in there, and there were holes in the roof so we were often literally rained on.

Much was amped up several notches for the film. Though everything was dialed up, we did a solid job of maintaining its crucial elements. Most of the original cast journeyed from our experimental outlet upstairs at the Royal Court to a rather large-scale motion picture. That consistency was crucial to keeping its integrity. I believe Sharman accepted a lower budget for the production itself to ensure that we were all brought along. We didn't mind; we all knew precisely what it was, and we weren't trying to turn Richard's B-movie rock 'n' roll musical into anything else.

We had picked up some new faces along the way, and we were very lucky in that regard. Meat Loaf—a real force of nature, with no confidence problem whatsoever—had been involved since we landed in LA, and Susan Sarandon and Barry Bostwick were newly cast for the film. Both Susan and Barry were brilliant at playing the naive babes in the wood while also understanding the irony underlying the premise and the nuances underpinning the absurdity of the whole thing. If memory serves, they were an item at the time, and one of them came and brought the other along...I'm not sure who led that. Probably Barry. Steve Martin originally auditioned to play Brad, which would have been great fun, but the part went to Barry, who was the better choice (in my opinion).

I had casually met Susan through friends from the crew in LA. She didn't mean to audition, but she was at the studio anyways, was convinced to read a scene, and it was clear that she would make the perfect Janet. The hang-up was that Susan was convinced she couldn't hold a tune. I think they asked her to sing "Happy Birthday" or something for the audition, just to see if she could hit basic notes. For what it's worth, I thought she had a very sweet voice. Not enormous power or control, perhaps. But she certainly has a *voice*. She was a great asset, both to the film and to my life.

She and Barry seemed to easily fall into step with the rest of the cast, which wouldn't have been easy to do. Plus, the American naivete you see in their characters felt very authentic and fresh, because it was real. Unfortunately, Susan did get very sick from the cold. There was, of course, the rain factor, plus we had to do a number of shots while drenched (after the pool scenes) and both Susan and Barry were practically nude for much of the film, so that wasn't terribly comfortable for them. Then again, that brand of discomfort was kind of perfect for playing Brad and Janet. And their (initially) straight-edge characters were offset by the extremely motley set of Transylvanians, who were—for the most part—notably high and ready for anything at any time. It didn't hurt that they were all cast for being extraordinarily good-looking.

For the most part, I stayed true to my original interpretation of Frank-N-Furter, though I made a few adjustments, which mainly had to do with trying to seduce the camera. The play was live and dynamic; onstage, my extravagance had to be more pronounced than it needed to be for the camera, which picks up on subtlety. I could glance at the camera for just a moment, and it would do the work of a much more deliberate pause onstage.

One learns a lot by playing a character on both stage and screen.

There were tweaks to the script here and there that made for great fun while filming. Perhaps the best upgrade was Frank's entrance through the elevator, which I suppose has become rather iconic. That was Jim's genius. He wanted it to be like Katharine Hepburn in *Suddenly, Last Summer* in the elevator... but in fishnet stockings. For the stage, I'd made my entrance right through the audience, which was sensational, and I got to feed off everybody's energy and—yes—*anticipation*. Of course, I had to generate that on my own for the film, but the elevator's slow progression achieved much of that tension for me.

In both the play and the film, Frank's strut does a lot of the work of establishing his power: the way he moves announces "HERE I AM." That didn't change. For the most part, that sort of bravado energy behind Frank is the same. The movement tells everyone around him who is in charge, whether onstage or onscreen. Entering the scene, in either version, never got old or tired for me. I had such fun ratcheting up that uncertainty and then exploding with energy.

Beyond the movements, the deliberate makeup choices for each character made a big difference. Our makeup designs were created by Pierre La Roche, who was well known—though perhaps not as well known as he *believed* he was—for glamming up Jagger and for creating the lightning bolt design for Bowie's Ziggy Stardust. In all fairness, he did a fabulous job; he made us look like extreme versions of our stage characters, which was exactly what we needed. He got it.

I was probably worked on the most, and Frank became a little more high fashion than I necessarily thought the character should be. (I suppose time and audience reception has suggested otherwise.) Pierre's Frank was a lot more polished, whereas I was careful to keep the integrity of a drag queen in my makeup, with smudged eyeliner. If that smudging made it to screen, I think Pierre would've stabbed himself in the eye with a mascara brush, just really go out with a bang.

For all his eccentricities, I enjoyed Pierre a lot; he was his own movie, in which you were invited to play a part but very carefully reminded that you could be disposed of at any time. He did a great job on Susan for the floor show, too. He fluffed her up in a big way, and I think she loved it, going from being the good girl to the vamp.

Our costume designer, Sue Blane, was absolutely superb in her own right. Everybody looked fabulous and absurd and everything we could have wanted—but she was also very true to the original. It was very important that she had been with us from the start. As I mentioned earlier, I was particularly grateful to her for fixing my shoes and making them into platforms, which allowed me to move with even more confidence. Frank can't have too much of it.

Perhaps the biggest difference between the film and the play happened offscreen, and pertained to the egos involved. In our stage production, the first musical number, "Science Fiction/Double Feature" was sung by Patricia Quinn (now Lady Stephens, after she married Maggie Smith's ex, Sir Robert Stephens), who plays Magenta in both versions. I don't remember why it was decided that Robert would take over and sing the part himself for the film. Patricia's lips are the ones used for the opening scene, and hers are the lips that are so recognizable to the branding of the film. She didn't hold back from expressing her displeasure; apparently, she almost quit over the decision, which would have been a real loss. I do know that singing that song had been what attracted her to the role, so I can imagine how enraged she might have been, though I wasn't involved in those conversations, blessedly.

Patricia and I had our own issues during the film, as it had taken her, as Magenta, a little while to come around in terms of ceding control to Dr. Frank-N-Furter. She got very competitive about the power that Frank held onstage. Back when we were in the theater, there'd been quite a discussion when Patricia and Nell realized they had juicy parts and weren't really responding to me (as Frank) in the way they should've been. One day, I had to stop and tell them right out: "I can't be powerful [as Frank] if my power is not reflected in the way you react to it, which is with subservience."

Now on set, the dynamics had shifted slightly, and instead of vying for the audience's attention from the stage, we were all focusing on the camera. There's this one scene in the movie with three people, including Patricia, in front of the lens, and she does this very slow turn of the head from one side to another, *knowing* it will rivet the camera. All of this happens while Frank is speaking, so, of course, I wasn't thrilled about it—but she definitely knew what she was doing. There are many ways to capture the camera's attention; sometimes, it's extremely outlandish behavior, but in her case, it was this very slowed-down and deliberate motion that totally drew the focus away from what was happening in the scene. Patricia has chutzpah, I'll give her that.

Thankfully, my friendship with Patricia and my other castmates has certainly outlasted that ego nonsense. And in some ways, the competition even pushed me to be better. I thought, "I better put you in your place, young lady," and ensured that Frank maintained his dominance over each scene as much as possible.

Aside from the clash of egos, the production ran into quite a few dramatic obstacles of its own. In the theater, Eddie makes his entrance through a Coca-Cola machine—which I loved. In the movie, though, Eddie, played by Meat Loaf, goes through a freezer on a motorcycle. I later go into the same freezer to retrieve the ax I used to murder Eddie. (Is it still a spoiler alert if it's been half a century?) Anyhow, his entrance was made more complex because he has to break through this sort of wax wall then pretty swiftly begin singing and playing "Hot Patootie–Bless My Soul."

Meat Loaf had no clue about driving a military-grade motorcycle, so a stuntman was brought in for the wide shots. For the close-ups, to make sure it looked like he was in motion, they put motorcycle handlebars and a windscreen on a wheelchair. At first, that seemed to work, but then somebody made the call to rig a camera up to the front as well. Well, gravity did its thing and the wheelchair flipped over, gashed up Meat Loaf's arm, and absolutely destroyed the camera. His stuntman tried to catch him, but in the process, *he* tripped up and broke his leg. Later on, in the scene when the motorcycle is winding its way around the room, the bike fell off the ledge and on top of the stunt rider—which was terribly dramatic, but he was fine, thank God. But the whole "Hot Patootie" scene was quite frenetic.

The kind of desperate, strung-out state that we all appear to be in by our respective ends? It was *very* real.

———

Once we wrapped on filming, I felt conflicted and hesitant about seeing the finished product. Initially, I struggled to really relate to the film as well. It was so important to me that my first film be a humdinger, and I felt that I'd brought off the character much better than I had. Upon release, my anxieties about it were realized when the movie absolutely bombed. Which was devastating. I couldn't say I was surprised, really; I knew that we had pushed it very far and that the wrong audience would take it the wrong way. But I also believed that there *was* the right audience out there for the film—and we just needed to find those people, somehow.

After its deeply disappointing reception, I moved on and, for a span of time, just presumed the whole experience was essentially behind me—until the midnight shows became such a phenomenon.

The movie could have easily disappeared into the recesses of cultural memory. But two key innovations turned the whole thing around. One came from a very clever young marketing man at Fox who invented the midnight circuit. After a few test showings around the country, Fox Marketing chose to air a midnight show at the ideal location of the Waverly cinema in Greenwich Village in New York. The second was that the audience very literally threw themselves into the show: first getting dressed up, yelling at the screen, and singing along—which evolved into bringing props and throwing things about. It turned the whole thing into a big party, one that everybody was invited to. The freakier, the better.

And that was also when I happened to have recently moved into a great apartment in New York, right behind the Waverly. It was a purpose-built apartment building and I lived on the top floor with access to the roof (and a lovely little garden). I'd found the apartment through Kathleen Turner, whom I'd met through my friend Holland Taylor. Kathleen's husband, Jay, was a major real estate guy in Manhattan and he mobilized his army to find me an apartment when I moved there. Voice actor Charlie Adler (no relation to Lou as far as I'm aware) does the most dead-on impersonation of Kathleen, because she met him with me at some sort of convention and she got his name wrong. You don't do that with Charlie because he can instantly go into his repertoire and just *kill*. But I was incredibly fortunate to cross paths with Kathleen and her husband when I did, and I'm thankful that they spent so much time and energy finding me a great place.

Anyhow, in a weird way, thanks to my building's fortuitous location, I got a front-row seat to one of the key venues from where the film's new life took off. It was quite weird, coming home around midnight or after the show and seeing people around the cinema dressed as me or any of the other characters.

By the time I finally went to see the show for myself, I was promptly thrown out for attempting to front as the "imposter" Tim Curry.

———

The fact that *Rocky Horror* is *still* showing at theaters at midnight, especially around Halloween, and has continued at the pace that it has, is nothing short of amazing to me. It helped a number of independent theaters survive in an age of mass consolidation and closure, and for that, I'm very proud. The astonishing subculture that gave it a second life with the midnight showings continues to thrive, with each generation finding a new way of connecting with this bizarre and beautiful production.

Over the years, the movie has been picked apart and analyzed ad nauseum, which is a tribute in itself. I don't have any wild revelations of my own; I just know it was a true adventure, and one I was blessed to have been a part of. That's not intended as a platitude, there's just not much more I can express about the film, other than to acknowledge my gratitude, particularly to Richard and to Jim, for going along with my "Tutti Frutti" audition and taking a chance on me.

People regularly refer to *The Rocky Horror Picture Show* as the ultimate cult classic, a term I came to despise, if for no other reason than it felt so overused as to be rendered meaningless. But its renewal, polarized opinions, and ongoing manifestations have made it deserving of that title. Even so, I'm inclined to focus more on it holding, or certainly sharing, the record for the longest-running theatrical release in film history, with limited releases still going as of this writing, in 2025. (Every new year, I keep being surprised by how long it's lasted!)

People often ask me for my opinion about why audiences keep coming back to this outrageous film. How has it proven to have such endurance, which has allegedly changed people's lives? What made it such a sensation?

Nobody fucking knows. Countless theories have been established, revised, and honed after fifty years of conjecture and consideration. The show itself was a very judicious mix of comic books and fifties rock 'n' roll and pop art, and I don't want to take anything away from Richard or Jim or what they created. But I also think it has lasted this long because of the hype and buzz and because it was a guaranteed party on Friday or Saturday nights at all these theaters that kept it running. It's just as good a party if you have a date as if you don't—and that has helped create and maintain the sense of community and of misfits coming together.

For the people who loved it and returned to see it multiple times on the stage—before the participation bit began—I believe the attraction was the wonder of that world. A world of permission. An escape from the limitations and judgments of the world we actually lived in.

Hardcore fans have approached me time and time again with a hankering to profoundly understand Frank-N-Furter or aspire to be him. I can only presume that they want to be as sexual, as confident, as powerful as the character. Maybe they just want to bang everybody in the room. Or, most likely, they want to be their weirdest self and be celebrated *because* of that weirdness—that's the Transylvanian standard.

I told a large crowd at a *Rocky Horror Picture Show* convention that I was comforted to know that there are so many people in this world sicker than I am. But the truth is that I sincerely hope it continues liberating people to be themselves. God knows it gave me license to forgo expectations and to embrace my contradictions. The entire scope of the experience was also, in many ways, among the most joyous times of my life.

Whatever it is that compels audiences of all stripes and all inclinations to continue showing up to shout at the screen and dance through the aisles in minimal clothing, it's astounding. May they continue to give themselves over to absolute pleasure for the next half century and beyond.

Chapter Eight

"An Artist Is Someone Who Makes Art Mean the Things He Does"

(Stoppard)

For all the cautionary warnings I received about being typecast, the roles that I took right after *Rocky Horror* really could not have been much further removed from my persona as Dr. Frank-N-Furter.

Quite soon after, I had the great privilege of appearing in both a film and a play adapted and written by the great Tom Stoppard. The TV film, produced for the BBC, was called *Three Men in a Boat*. It's an adaptation of Jerome K. Jerome's classic comic novel, chronicling the misadventures of three friends (and a dog) as they embark on a boating holiday along the River

Thames. I played Jerome K. Jerome, the sort of ringleader of
the starring triad, but a very different kind of ringleader than
Frank. I've often joked that, after playing so many eccentric
roles, I would rather like to play a bank clerk. On paper, Jerome
is the closest role I could find to achieve that, but he's quite an
upscale, complex bank clerk—not exactly dull but certainly not
an overtly sexualized Transylvanian. Quite the reverse, in fact.

Identifying the common humanity and bringing it to the
surface is how I've managed to inhabit all different kinds of
people or creatures, but it starts and ends with the words on
the page. A production by Stoppard offers a *lot* of words with
which to work, which contributed—in part—to why I felt rather
unsure of myself in the production. It was a very far cry from a
transvestite doctor attempting to create the perfect man. Still, I
found the challenge tantalizing.

For the role of Jerome K. Jerome, they cut my hair short and
dyed it blond. That somehow gave me a completely different
sense of myself, which I rather enjoyed. And I had great fun
doing *Three Men in a Boat*. For the majority of the filming, we
simply rode up the Thames, stopping every few miles.

Tom Stoppard and I became friendly during that film
because the majority of the cast and crew were staying in this
riverside hotel and we would all share a car to the location. I
was absolutely fascinated by him. On those car rides, he and I
bonded over our shared love of soul music and Motown, which
he would play in the car. We wouldn't croon along in unison
or anything like that, but I loved that we could appreciate the
music together.

Stoppard is an exceptional writer and has great command
of the language in his scripts, be they plays or adaptations.

I'd like to believe that one of the main reasons why Tom and I got along so well was because of our shared reverence for the words on the page. The greatest ingredient in the secret sauce of my career is that I always read the fucking script—and closely. Anything I want to know should be somewhere in the text, so for each of my roles, I begin by reading through the script very thoroughly until I get an idea of how I want to play it. Then I show up, I run through it, and I listen to my director's feedback.

Somewhere in that process, I typically uncover where my character's tendencies align with my own nature. Once I find that humanity, I keep digging, especially once I am at the stage of engaging with other characters, which is often where *their* natures are revealed. My vetting process for scripts has always involved seeking that connection or compassion in whichever character I'm considering—and only taking on the role if I can find it. This, in turn, has contributed greatly to my resume of very non-boring characters.

I was actually pitched the gig for *Three Men in a Boat* while I was still living in LA at Sunset Tower. It was Stephen Frears himself, the director of the film, who called me.

"How would you like to come back to England and play Jerome K. Jerome?"

I was familiar with the work. "What makes you think that I could play a Victorian bank clerk?" I asked.

"Well, after Frank-N-Furter, I think you could probably play anything. Plus, you're funny," he said. It was hugely encouraging, because I admired Stephen quite a lot (and still do), and his confidence in me felt both flattering and affirming. So as soon as I had been offered the opportunity, I jumped at it.

A film about three young blades, working in banks in the late nineteenth century and deciding to venture out of London on a skiff to stop at various places along the Thames, was certainly an adjustment. The pace was completely different than what I'd just experienced with *The Rocky Horror Show*. Modifying my rhythm and adhering to the language was a rigorous, albeit welcome, challenge.

One of the best parts of *Three Men in a Boat* was that it was shot during a beautiful, idyllic English summer in 1975, and every day we got in a boat and sat in the sun and glided down the river. It was a lovely time. I got the additional bonus of acting alongside Michael Palin, of Monty Python fame, and Stephen Moore—two men whose work I greatly admired and respected.

Stephen was very funny and generous, without a competitive bone in his body. Michael, though, always had to be a touch competitive—he had come up from those Oxford comic shows and then with the Pythons, among whom you basically had to spill blood if you wanted to get your bit on the screen. Despite that, I don't think he harbors a mean thought for anybody. He has a sunny disposition and is a damn fine actor. He's also a genuinely lovely person, with great intelligence and integrity. The rapport among the three of us was also excellent: they both made me laugh a lot with their clever, unexpected asides and spontaneous wit. Honestly, it felt a bit like a holiday, given the beautiful scenery that surrounded us and the privilege of shooting outside.

While at first a bit wary as to how I would approach this new character, it helped that Jerome K. Jerome—who had written the book at the turn of the century—was so refreshingly ordinary, as was the world that surrounded him. Or I suppose I should say: ordinary *to an extent*. For his true nature, especially when adapted by Stoppard, was seasoned with a pinch of narcissism and panache, as can be found in one of my favorite lines of his: "I leant with careless grace upon the hitcher, in an attitude suggestive of agility and strength, and threw an air of tender wistfulness into my expression, mingled with a touch of cynicism, which I am told suits me..."

It was a fitting role for me at a fitting time. The characters were seeking to escape the business of London for a few weeks, which was a very attractive proposition for me. In many ways he was the perfect off-ramp for me to play after inhabiting Frank for so many years. My time spent as Jerome was brief, but it served as an ideal reminder that I was capable of stretching beyond *Rocky* and, perhaps more importantly, enjoyed doing so.

———

After *Rocky Horror* and *Three Men in a Boat*, there wasn't a stampede to employ me. Directors and audiences didn't yet know the range of what I could do. To be fair, I didn't yet know, either; I was still quite a novice and had yet to reach thirty. Thankfully, I had formed a connection with Stoppard, and I believe he must have been the one to put forth the idea to audition me for his highly complicated, intellectual play *Travesties*.

Despite our connection, even I was surprised to land a role. It was my first original Stoppard to be performed on the stage, and is a play in which there are many, *many* words. The sheer density of the language and the importance of hitting the mark with every word makes it a very easy play to fuck up. Tom asks a great deal from the actors and, by way of following along, from the audience.

One of the most incredible things about Tom is that he was born in Czechoslovakia; he and his family fled to Singapore (and later India) during World War II, before his mother married an officer in the British army and moved the family back to England. All this to say: English is not Tom's native tongue, and yet it's a language he's long burnished and revered. He sees language as a real responsibility, which I believe it is, and that sense of duty is reflected in his work. Because of this, and the density of this play in particular, it was intimidating to take on the role Tom had in mind for me, knowing (or presuming) that my reputation could hinge upon my performance. But that's all part of the thrill—and I was eager to prove that I was ready to handle the abundance and precision of his language, night after night, for the entire run.

A lot of nonsense is presumed about classical English training for theater actors. One aspect of that reputation is accurate: the emphasis on faithfully delivering the writer's language. It's the foundation of discipline in English acting—holding respect for language, and conveying it in clean, accurate verse. It's so important, as an actor, to get it exactly right. It baffles me when I'm onstage with people who don't appreciate or respect the dialogue they've been given. That was impressed upon me very early. I admire and adhere to that practice, and I certainly needed it to pull off my part in *Travesties*.

Travesties tells the story of what happens when Lenin, James Joyce, and Tristan Tzara meet in Zurich toward the end of the First World War. I found it a dazzling idea to get all those minds together onstage. I played Tzara—essentially the publicist of the Dada movement. He wasn't much of an artist himself—in fact, his work was extremely resistible—but he proved himself to be massively influential as the very strong energy behind the movement. He also organized the Dadaists, starting in Zurich, then on to Paris.

The play is a comedy of ideas, weaving together themes of art and dissident movements through Lenin's politics, Joyce's writing, and the Dadaists' work. But the whole play is viewed from the perspective of Henry Carr, a man in the British consular service. James Joyce, who wrote much of *Ulysses* in Zurich, approaches Carr to play Algernon in *The Importance of Being Earnest*. They have a massive row because Carr wants to be reimbursed for a pair of trousers. Joyce sues him, then writes him into *Ulysses* as a rather rude and ineffective private.

The play itself was based off Carr's highly questionable memoirs, in which Lenin, Joyce, and Tzara meet regularly. But as Carr was also involved with the production of Oscar Wilde's *The Importance of Being Earnest*, excerpts of that work are embedded throughout, making it consistently unclear what's happening and in which world. It was, of course, a highly ambitious endeavor to write such a play, and it's terribly clever. Especially as I was still in my twenties, I remember feeling a huge responsibility to honor Stoppard's ambitious work.

An actor called John Wood, a master of language in his own right, played the part of Henry Carr. John was an incredibly skilled actor and not just a little intimidating. He made it clear that he would have preferred to work with somebody with more of a rep or resume than I had at the time. John was a heavyweight who was riding a very respectable trajectory through his acting career, and he didn't want it to be threatened because of some kid.

I have no desire to disparage other actors. We were all doing the best we could. But I would be remiss to mischaracterize working with John in *Travesties*, because in reality, acting together was the most significant challenge I had yet faced in my career. When we started rehearsals, which are always a bit of a hothouse to begin with, I found him unusually greedy and hubristic, in addition to being openly hostile toward me whether we were in character or out. John never stated his skepticism about me explicitly; it was just evident based on how poorly he treated me. He deliberately changed the blocking onstage both during rehearsals and shows, which confused me and had the potential to take me right out of character. He never even looked at my eyes; he only ever looked at my shoulder—which was incredibly disorienting. And he took the dialogue at a tremendous speed, which I had to keep up with, which was a hugely beneficial experience and taught me a great deal about pace and its importance.

When I'm onstage, I know almost exactly how much air I displace. What I mean is, if I sweep my arm in any direction, that's the air that I'm displacing, or occupying. I do everything I possibly can to occupy the air around me onstage, but still, it needs to be earned. Onstage, you are performing in a sort of vacuum. Which is not the case on set, because then it's about being overheard by a camera. Regardless, mixing up the carefully staged blocking had the potential to really knock me off my game and out of my element.

One night, John even threw a glass of whiskey across the stage. He used to have a glass of whiskey every intermission, and on this particular occasion, he brought it with him onstage and lobbed it across the stage because he was angry for a miscue or something. He had a very short temper, John did.

I do have to give him credit, however, for warming to me and later apologizing. I'll never forget the moment I stood beside him during a curtain call, and as we joined hands, John turned to me and murmured, "Well, I *suppose* you're getting better." It may seem like a small gesture, but I appreciated it at the time.

Years later, he apologized to me more explicitly, which came as a real shock. He'd invited me and a great friend to stay with him in his restored, rather beautiful house in the country, which was an odd invitation in the first place and certainly not one I was expecting. He apologized for being disrespectful. I wasn't entirely convinced by his gesture, but at the time I was grateful and I expect a little triumphant (which is, I know, unbecoming).

Either way, it did not fuck up my performance. The play went on to win a Tony, and Wood took one home as well, for Best Actor. I think I resolved our dissonance at the time by convincing myself that being combative was part of the deal with actors and that I should get used to it. However I rationalized it, it served me well at the time. I was damned determined to prove my skills, and Wood's lack of faith in me gave me that much more impetus to actually pull it off.

Though I rarely prepare exhaustively, I made an exception for *Travesties*. I literally shut myself in a hotel room at a place called Blake's for three weeks to learn my part. That was not ideal for my mental health, in retrospect, but I was frightened of failure. It would have been disastrous had I not known my lines flawlessly. Getting them emblazoned into my head bore fruit from the first days of rehearsal, because I never wasted anyone's time—at least, not when it came to knowing the script.

The play did enormously well, critically and commercially. The 1974 performance in London's West End ran along with the Royal Shakespeare Company season. Afterward, we were transferred to Broadway, where the play continued through 1976. Among other gifts, the consistent paycheck enabled me to pay that outstanding balance at the Algonquin in five-dollar bills.

When we went to New York to open the play, I was excited to reconnect with friends who lived in the city. One was an actress called Joan Hackett, who had an apartment on the second floor of a building at Ninetieth and Central Park West. She rented it to me for a super-reasonable amount. It was a swanky, splendid address for me and my extremely limited pocket, and made the whole adventure seem far more glamorous than anything I had earned per se.

The first night of *Travesties* in New York, Rita Moreno confused me for Tom Stoppard and approached me afterward to say, "You must be very proud. It is such a great play you've written!"

"Thank you very much, Rita," I responded, not bothering to correct her. I smiled genially and threw my arm around her as though we were old pals. After all, it *was* a fabulous production, and being confused for Stoppard was a mix-up that I felt very comfortable playing along with.

Among the great, formative gifts of being cast in *Travesties* was being introduced to theater director Peter Wood, who became a massively influential mentor and friend to me. Peter was a dashing figure whose faith in me was especially meaningful in those post-*Rocky* years. He recognized something in me, though I'm not sure what it was. We both loved the countryside in the West of England, where he lived. I'd visit on the occasional weekend, and we'd take long walks. Not hikes, mind you—lovely *walks*. Let it be known that I have never been an intrepid hiker. Our walks were just about keeping our eyes open to the beautiful nature around us.

Peter often surprised me. He would cast me as Shakespeare in *Will Shakespeare* in 1978, which I hadn't expected, because it was another significant leap from the roles I had played. But I quickly got on with it, because Peter was directing it, and I gauged that even though he wanted to encourage me, he wouldn't have cast me unless he truly thought I was capable of pulling it off. He relentlessly gave me opportunities, and largely thanks to his assuredness, I believe I proved myself strong enough to do justice to the roles in which he cast me.

Peter's support wasn't limited to my theatrical endeavors. After taking me under his wing and observing my work ethic, Peter encouraged me to pursue joy. He was interested in the finer things in life—particularly food, but also objects, behavior, and general well-being. I needed to hear his encouragement, though I honestly didn't know what he meant when he advised as much. I can't call back his exact message, but the gist of it was something along the lines of: "Don't kick joy aside because of the work. You have a life to live, and you must live it."

Of course, he was right.

While I was in New York, Peter Wood introduced me to another early hero and influential mentor, Peter Shaffer. They shared a name, age, general demeanor, and propensity for collecting blue and white china, a habit I later adopted myself. (I find it highly amusing to imagine somebody back in 1810 in Staffordshire, or somewhere in the middle of England, imagining what China was like and getting it hilariously wrong.)

Shaffer was also British, but he'd lived in New York for a long time, and made me feel instantly welcome in a place not widely known for opening its arms. A supersmart, literate person, Shaffer had recently started working on writing *Amadeus*, an innovative look at the life of Mozart (I would later play the titular role on Broadway). He was a gentle, hysterically funny, generous friend who was quite kind to me, and who truly eased my transition into living in America.

I've always been very driven, but as work ramped up, I was mindful about keeping Peter Wood's cautionary advice in mind. He had perhaps noted that I was taking myself too seriously, and that I was not giving myself space to enjoy the fruits of my labor. So I really tried, based on his advice, to be more conscientious about not kicking joy aside. Working very hard as a performer always came naturally. I wasn't trying to prove anything; I just didn't know how to do it any other way. Pausing to relax and enjoy my life was something I had to do much more intentionally.

Luckily, I was settling into a new city that demands and enables very hard work *and* very hard play.

Chapter Nine

"I Do the Rock"

I HAD A LOT GOING ON DURING THE HEARTIEST NEW YORK phase of my life, particularly as the late seventies rolled into the eighties. At one point I was working on a film, a record, and a play, often all in the same day. I was high on all of it and was also absolutely exhausted—but equally, I recognized that it was a fulfillment of everything I'd always wanted to do: all those art forms, all at once.

I can't claim that I was merely relying exclusively on a good night's sleep to get through those days. It *was* New York in the eighties. Once I had settled there, I embraced the whole scene, which included my taking to cocaine like a duck to water. The stuff in New York was much more dangerous than what was back home in England, because it was phenomenally pure. It came right from South America. My dealer, a member of the string section in the New York Philharmonic, was superb: charming, and so sweet. He used to get lovely pure blow; I never felt like it was cut with anything. He was too savvy to carry it around in a case or anything cinematic like that, which was a bit disappointing. But I was still an excellent customer. Like smoking, cocaine was something that I was terribly good at.

And so, I hit the ground running in New York. My thorough coke habit assisted me in becoming a lyricist and getting on with my music career, as well as all the acting. That dangerous habit was of a time and place, however. I honestly felt that by the time I left New York, I had snorted most of Peru—and I was able to cut the habit relatively easily.

I liked myself as a New Yorker. I was a bit tougher. Sometimes living there can toughen people too much, or make them trust people less. It's good to have that experience, though, because it means that you can apply it when necessary anywhere else.

For a number of reasons, it's quite hard for me to remember New York very crisply. It was always colored by whatever work I was doing, and if I had a moment when I wasn't onstage or onscreen, I was rather occupied trying to write songs and music for the first time.

I'd always been a singer; singing as a young boy in my father's services had been my introduction to being a performer, and many of my pivotal roles have relied on my confidence that I was versatile enough to both sing and act. Because of this, I was lucky enough to have a go at being a rock 'n' roll star after *Rocky Horror Picture Show* had come out. Lou Adler agreed to sign me and give me a chance at a second career. I went to his house with one of my agents who specialized in music, and we sat in his garden and negotiated a deal right there. My representative had written out our parameters and ideals on a yellow legal notepad, and Lou took the pad from him and went through the notes very closely, which was very smart of him and less of a savvy move from my agent. In retrospect, those negotiations were sort of a preview of what the record business was going to be like.

Nonetheless, we struck a deal, and not long after we signed the papers, I went into the studio and got quite involved. In the beginning, I was laser-focused on the music. It was thrilling. I wanted to do nothing else for the foreseeable future. Of course, I would have loved to have broken through as a singer. Alas... I did not.

Lou and the other producers found it difficult to establish a style or pick a genre for me. I take the responsibility for that: I didn't make it easy. My band and I covered the waterfront, and I was interested in everything that was coming up at the time. Disco was very big then, so we had a handful of disco-inspired songs. I even covered a few by Patti LaBelle's group, including "Far as We Felt Like Goin'." (Years later, I bumped into her at one of my favorite restaurants, Da Silvano, and I told her I'd covered it. She couldn't have been less interested.) I also sort of rapped on one of the tracks, by imagining talking to people on the dance floor.

Lou was not especially enthralled by my range of music, as most record producers want to be able to sum up the genre of a given album—but I've never been interested in being conveniently placed into a single category, and it felt new and important to experiment with all of the different kinds of music that inspired me.

Over the years, Lou had made a ton of very good records and worked with phenomenally successful artists—notably, the Mamas & the Papas and Carole King, and he had even done a bit of work with the legendary Sam Cooke. I knew how lucky I was that he had any interest in adding me to that list. Lou has a strong, assertive personality and he had some great ideas as a producer; we just had different notions of how best to achieve them. For example, I covered "Baby Love" by the Supremes. He had the idea of getting Tower of Power—the amazing funk group of very energetic horn players—to play on it. But I'd imagined the song sounding a lot slower, almost as a throaty ballad, so that's how I played it.

However passionately I felt about it, I was green in the recording studio. After laying down a few tracks, Lou either saw diminishing potential or just lost interest and handed the album over to John Phillips from the Mamas & the Papas. I wasn't very happy about being handed off to somebody else without much say, but I didn't make a big fuss about it, hoping that Lou sensed some kind of chemistry that might prove to be a stroke of genius. But no. Unfortunately, John was quite wrong for me in the end, though it wasn't his fault. In fact, one could go so far as to argue that I was quite wrong for John. But then again, this isn't his memoir.

Lou gave me a lot of room to explore and make my own mark, but it was also the time of the Laurel Canyon sound. Soft rock and folk, heartfelt confessionals and declarations set to a gently strummed guitar…that's simply not how I play music, nor is it what I was listening to. Joni Mitchell's a glaring, brilliant, inimitable exception to the rule. I adore her work and revere her music, because in addition to being courageous, her songs are poetry.

While pursuing my musical side, I had great times with Carole King, who was very kind to me. Through Lou, we were on the same label, so she used to invite me over to her house to jam. She'd regularly have sessions with some fairly big-shot musicians and singers. I was too scared to sing in front of such talent, thank God. One woman who was memorably fearless in that category was Cher. Though I knew my own limits, I managed to relax quite easily, primarily because Carole was so open and generous and made everybody feel welcome. I also struck up a friendship with her daughter, Louise Goffin. She was a bit of a prodigy herself, and was recording at about the same time as I was. She is a rather good musician in her own right and made a couple of albums. She was genuinely delightful company. (I trust she still is.)

Once established in that scene, connections came quite easily. Carly Simon and James Taylor, who were married at the time, became good friends of mine. I remember one night in particular when Carly and I went out on the town in New York. It was a night that feels very representative of that stage of my life and of that era. She wanted to go to Studio 54 but was nervous about going alone because Steve Rubell, who ran the club, was selectively not allowing celebrities to come in (largely just to prove that he could turn away anyone). Carly didn't want any confrontation like that. I agreed to join her, and she picked me up in a limo. She needn't have worried; as soon as we pulled up, we were waved right through the huge throng outside.

After being welcomed graciously, we were escorted up to the DJ booth, which was the smart place to be. Truman Capote was deejaying—one of his favorite things to do.

"Truman, I want you to meet some people," Rubell said.

Truman looked at Carly and noted, in his signature nasal tone, "Oh. I knew your *faaaaather.*" Then he looked at me in, well…let's just call it an entirely *different* kind of way.

Soon after the introductions, we were ushered down to the basement, which was unofficially known as a den for bad behavior. There were bowls of coke out on the table. We enjoyed plenty of that, though Carly didn't really partake—I don't think she liked that particular high very much. But Truman sure did. At some point, Andy Warhol joined us as well. He had a bit of a thing for me, so that was all right. Eventually we staggered out into the night, or early day, and couldn't find the driver, which is the way it goes with those types of outings.

That was what New York was like, from the sunset of the seventies into the early eighties. That time period also overlapped with the all-inclusive *Rocky Horror* resurgence that was occurring simultaneously. There was a wonderful hum and energy in the city, filth and vices and all. I came to feel like a real New Yorker, though natives to the city would no doubt balk at such a claim.

I was ever a vagabond drinker, but stopped using blow when it grew apparent that it wasn't appropriate any longer. Blessedly I wasn't in its grasp—by which I mean I never craved it *desperately.* After quitting, I'd still indulge in the occasional line or a bump here and there, then would regret it instantly, because I didn't actually enjoy the drug—no matter how smart I thought I was while on it.

"Well, fuck, *that* wasn't a good idea" would usually be my first thought.

I wasn't especially addicted to the city, either, though the pace of living inspired a lot of creativity and proved a marvelously stimulating place to be when I was writing songs. Meeting the standards for performers in the city also ensured that I stayed sharp enough to work across multiple genres at once.

———

The recording studio presented unique challenges for me, as opposed to being onstage or in front of a camera, where I had more confidence and experience. Had I been more familiar with the lay of the land, I would have been a little freer with my improvisation, and also in the way that I directed others. Initially, I felt fairly constricted because the band (largely, expensive studio musicians) and the producers were old hands and notably unconvinced by my abilities. Or it certainly felt that way.

I never quite gained the self-assurance that I was coming across as intended. Then again, when I said one song didn't feel quite right and tried to illustrate what I was going for, the guitar player deadpanned, "The musical term that you are searching for is...'slower.'"

A bit crushing, really.

In any case, the music I made with Lou was not released—at least, not until much later, when a few of the songs we'd recorded were included on an album entitled... *From the Vaults*, inspired by a quote from *Rocky Horror*. At the time, feeling like it was all for naught was immensely frustrating. In the end, it was just as well for the wider listening public. I'm still fond of a few of the tunes but the albums, overall, were not great achievements.

Fortunately, music wasn't completely out of the cards, and things started taking off once I started recording for A&M

Records, especially after co-owner Jerry Moss and producer
Bob Ezrin came into the picture. We ended up making three
albums together (*Read My Lips*, *Fearless*, and *Simplicity*), all
written and produced around when the seventies were crashing
into the eighties (or flowing into the eighties, depending on the
morning).

That second album, *Fearless*, reached number 53 on the *Billboard* 200 in the US, and one of the songs, "I Do the Rock,"
even made it onto the *Billboard* Hot 100. Back when we were
writing and recording for the record, I'd been reading a biogra-
phy of a family of literary siblings called the Sitwells, who came
from a line of British aristocrats. I was fascinated by the eldest
sister, Edith. She was one of the last Victorians, really, and had
this impossibly high forehead, which probably owed something
to a razor. As much as possible, she tried to look like a medieval
saint, with flowing clothes and her slim, long-fingered hands
and this sulky, sullen expression that made it seem like she
was always sitting for a portrait by Giotto. She was very grand.
Edith and her siblings were all poets, and she used to host these
readings at her home on Moscow Road in Kensington where
she'd invite all of these aspiring poets to come and share their
work, and then they'd have endless discussions about the poems.

Anyways, one day, when my friend and collaborator Michael
Kamen and I stepped into the funny little studio we used to
record in sometimes, he started playing a good riff, and I just
started improvising what I imagined Edith and her siblings
might be like at one of those readings. I knew nobody would
know who the fuck any of them were—and I loved that. And
what do you know, it ended up being somewhat of a turnta-
ble hit.

In the summer of '79, I went on the road with my band to promote *Fearless* and had a spectacular time. I especially appreciated my bass player, who was a great guy and big in every way: tall, fleshy, with an enormous personality. He wasn't sexy at all, but, man, he was a really good bass player and a really good person. We used to rehearse in a rather cheap studio. Every time somebody bought some coke, instead of contributing, he put that amount of money in his pocket and saved it. Eventually, he saved up enough to actually buy the studio, if that gives any indication of how much partying was going on.

We did a sort of winter tour, then a summer tour round through the States. The latter felt like visiting a series of swimming pools across America. In Phoenix, Jerry Moss asked me to open for Peter Frampton at a massive arena. I was terrified and realized that if I wanted to make it work, I had to basically act as if I were a caricature of myself, exaggerating everything in front of the arenas I played. In the end, I managed it...to the response of a single pair of hands clapping.

Then we all trekked over to Germany, where my albums had performed rather well and I'd accumulated a surprising volume of fans (though whether it was for my music or *Rocky Horror*, I'm not sure). All in all, the tour was smashing, with one notable exception that's very cringeworthy to recall. It was a rather nightmarish concert in Berlin, where I was utterly smashed. We could never find coke in Germany, so I'd substituted one vice for another, and my band and I drank heavily ahead of the show, which was a grand mistake on my part. So much so that I gracelessly fell off the stage in the middle of a performance, after far too much brandy. That was less than endearing. The show went on and all that, but I had left my dignity on the floor.

Touring as a musician is very different than being on the road with a production. As an actor, I tended to take planes, then stay in one place for at least a month. With the band, though, we toured in a bus, which we slept in and pretty much lived in. When the show was over at the end of the night, we'd essentially crawl back into it, grateful to be off our feet. I was surrounded by musos, all of whom were well-versed in that lifestyle and pace. Though I was well-suited to a lifestyle that requires jostling between constant motion (going from gig to gig) and delayed inertia (waiting to get onstage, a period particularly ripe for overindulgence and drinking, if only just to pass the time), there was still a learning curve. I knew I had to assert my personality, for the band and for the audience. But what made this different than asserting myself as an actor is that I didn't have a character to hide behind. It was just me up there—although, I suppose, in a way, you invent a character for yourself in that capacity as well. Especially in front of a band.

People didn't quite know what to expect from me as a rock 'n' roll artist. I can't say that I knew what to expect from myself, either. But I did love getting the chance to cross paths with so many talented musicians. Sometimes I'd nod at legends in the studio, other times I'd meet them at parties and decide to make some music together. The latter was the case with Ronnie Spector, the iconic "bad girl of rock 'n' roll." We were in New York City and I went over to her apartment that was somewhere downtown, in a more industrial area. We had discussed writing a song together, but that never happened. We composed a… different kind of song? I mean, we just sort of blew our minds: I got so shit-faced I literally couldn't speak. I couldn't even say goodbye, I just kind of vaguely moved my arm in a waving motion and left.

I presume it was great fun, but it never feels that way the following morning, especially when there's not a song or anything really lasting to show for it. Though I suppose I'm writing about it in my memoir now, so there you go.

———

When the music was over, it was over. The less lyrical way to phrase that is that my professional music career was brought to an end when my contract with A&M closed out and they were not moved to extend it. That was a rather blatant sign. But I accepted that that phase had run its course and so I went off to get involved in a different production. I wouldn't say I was entirely ready to be done with it; it was just very evident that trying to be both a musician and an actor would only run me into the ground—and swiftly. I knew I was a better actor, and also knew music would always be with me. Several of my forthcoming roles, in fact, would depend on that ability to sing and feel the music.

I've come around to feeling proud of that stage of my life, of giving it a go as a musician and of people paying to hear or see me sing. It was a wild era that ushered in wild nights and busy days. But when I first stopped recording, I couldn't listen to the radio for about two and a half years. Doing so was just too painful, I think. I would compare myself and get stuck in a trap of self-indulgent debate that serves nobody and does nothing. I knew the lifestyle would not have been sustainable for me in the long term; even so, something about hearing new music saddened me, as it would make me remember that I had thoroughly disconnected myself from something I had once felt so passionate about and driven to do.

To this day, I very rarely listen to any of my albums, though there's a song I wrote that still lifts my spirits. It's called "Working on My Tan," and is a sort of vaguely reggae-leaning tune, which I wrote in the hopes that it might be a big summer single. The song was inspired by that midsummer feeling, but we never really nailed down a great arrangement for it. I just couldn't come up with the ideal way to end it—a problem I've always had with my music. I'm still trying to improve it in my mind, still trying to land on the perfect ending for that song.

I'll let you know when I find it.

Chapter Ten

"I Can't Rewrite What's Perfect"

(*Amadeus*)

W HEN I FIRST WALKED IN THE FRONT DOOR OF PETER
Shaffer's apartment, there was a table in the foyer dis-
playing a stack of books he was reading at the time. Walking
into the main room, I felt like I was being embraced by the
tall bookshelves and the literature they held. Though it was
an amazing penthouse on Eighty-Ninth and Riverside on the
Upper West Side, with a stunning terrace that looked out onto
the Hudson and Riverside Park, the energy of the space within
wasn't stifling or overly swanky. Artfully and intentionally
designed, it was the type of place where one felt immediately at

home. At least that was my initial reaction, and I continued to feel that way each time I visited.

Once I was accustomed to life in New York, I developed a routine of going over to his house pretty much every Sunday evening. Shaffer was a great chef, and whenever I came over, he would cook a proper English roast—the type of suppers I missed most. I love all kinds of food, but there's a comfort that comes with a hearty English meal. A lot of our food is shit—it's not exactly a secret—but when cooked well, stuff like steak and liver and bacon pies are delicious.

Shaffer certainly knew what he was doing, so he'd cook up a delicious leg of lamb or a chicken, a duck, a goose, or something extravagant and very British. He used to get quite ambitious whenever I came over. I'd be treated to all the fixings: plenty of gorgeous potatoes and side dishes of one kind or another, which he enjoyed cooking more than anything. He could also shake a mean cocktail—back then, I think we were rather fond of Manhattans (rather appropriate, too, given the setting). If memory serves, I would begin laughing from the moment I walked in the door until closing it behind me to leave, because Peter was one of the funniest people I knew, and our senses of humor were perfectly aligned. I admired him greatly as a playwright, and appreciated that Peter Wood had introduced us.

He also wrote one hell of a role for me.

I first got wind of it through his boyfriend, Robert Leonard, who was an operatic vocal coach. Over cocktails one evening, while Shaffer was in the kitchen, Robert leaned over to me in an almost conspiratorial fashion and said, "Peter's writing a *wonderful* part for you."

"Don't say that," I insisted, "because it'll never happen."

To my great fortune, it did. I received a call from Peter Hall, the director, asking if I would come audition for the part of Wolfgang Mozart in his new play, *Amadeus*. The narrative was centered around the rivalry between Mozart and Salieri. In the eighteenth century, Salieri was the most successful composer in Europe—and yet he's not at all commonly known today, certainly not in comparison to Mozart. His work fell out of favor very quickly. Salieri starts the play by telling the audience that he's poisoned Mozart, setting an insidious tone.

I agreed enthusiastically to the audition, but as soon as I hung up the phone, I was immediately seized by nerves. By this point in time, it had been about five years since I'd performed in a play. Theater work is a muscle, and I was anxious about having gone so long without exercising it. I remember sitting in the front row of the Ethel Barrymore Theatre, talking to the director and staring at the elegant stage, trying to figure out how I was going to walk up there gracefully, then perform the act required, which included jumping onto a chair, without betraying the intensity of the anxiety I felt.

There was also a bit too much of me at the time (perhaps a result of those indulgent dinners at Shaffer's), and I feared that I would displace too much air up onstage. Imagining delivering my lines from up there made it suddenly feel very far away, like some distant, daunting summit I wasn't ready to climb.

Knowing I still had a job to do, I took a very deep breath and got on with it. The rest is a blur, but by some miracle, I managed to secure the part, and was cast alongside Ian McKellen, who would play Salieri, Mozart's rival, as he had done in London.

In 1979, the play premiered at the National Theatre in London, and the role of Mozart initially went to Simon Callow. He was directed to play the character in a kind of cartoonish manner, who would sort of skip around the stage impishly. The thinking behind it was that he was behaving as though it was happening in Salieri's mind, and Salieri saw Mozart as a figure who existed far beneath him. But I didn't want to perform the character from that angle, from Salieri's presumed perception. I also wasn't particularly interested in the comedic angle; instead, I wanted to bring out more of Mozart's emotional depth and complicated humanity. Peter had this idea that Mozart is this gifted child who enjoys shocking people, but at his core, he feels things quite deeply, and, as it is with every gifted child, yearns for a mentor to guide him into adulthood. I sought to bring that nuance to the stage.

So when *Amadeus* transferred to Broadway in 1980 and I secured the role, I decided to play it quite differently. Nobody seemed to mind. We opened in Washington, and Peter revised it significantly while we were there. As a result, we never knew which version of a scene we were going to play, which was very challenging indeed. But extremely exciting, too. He wasn't afraid to be an artisan, Peter, and—ever the perfectionist—was seeking to land on the exact right version. He wanted the play to explore the nature of genius, because he knew personally how fucking hard it is to write, whether it's music or words. He was also particularly fascinated with Mozart's relationship with his father, and wanted to explore its full complexity.

Peter Hall ran the National Theatre in England, so he was familiar with my work. He's another Peter who has been very kind to me, and had confidence in me that I was never sure was entirely founded. Peter founded and then led the Royal Shakespeare Company for many years, as a sort of whiz kid in his twenties throughout the 1950s and '60s; for example, he was the first person to recognize the brilliance of Samuel Beckett's *Waiting for Godot*. Shortly after the National Theatre was invented and inaugurated, he succeeded Laurence Olivier as its leader, in 1973. So his reputation was well established by the time he brought *Amadeus* over to Broadway. He did everything he could to ensure that I felt secure, but there's no way for it to not be at least a bit intimidating when you're cast as an iconic figure like Mozart.

This was also during a time when I teetered very close to a potentially serious burnout. The cocaine span of my life had slowed significantly after my rock 'n' roll career ended. There was a bit of a saving grace in that. Not that the combination of trying to be a singer while keeping up with a regular cocaine habit is very conducive anyways.

But once I started *Amadeus*, I was still doing a line or two in the middle of the day with my friend Michael, who was my arranger and songwriting partner. This was some very pure, *very* potent blow, so much so that it hadn't worn off entirely when it came time to do the show one night. I made my entrance and began a scene. Ian could see that though I was delivering my lines, I was not in total command of myself. He communicated as much by raising an eyebrow and giggling, just kind of letting me know that he knew I wasn't totally right, I guess. It may not seem that disastrous, but it was a horrible experience and ensured that I would no longer combine recreation with work so recklessly. It wasn't the raised eyebrow or the judgment. It was just not being able to have control onstage, especially when it came to a role for which I cared deeply.

The parallels between my own experience and Salieri's didn't escape me. Shaffer's play is about a man of genius who has no

self-concern, no control, and no discipline—a man who behaves
so stupidly that he drives himself into the ground and dies in an
attic, eaten up by jealousy. In writing the character through this
angle, Peter was essentially asking God why he would allow this
to happen to such a genius, and it's certainly a cautionary tale of
what can happen when one surrenders too completely to their
vices.

I was still writing music for my album *Simplicity* when I
started rehearsing for *Amadeus*. I'd always be either writing lyr-
ics and humming a tune in the studio or in my little loft in the
Village. It was quite strange to spend most of the day recording
a contemporary album, then put on a different hat (from the
eighteenth century) and go become Mozart. I think it helped
me understand him a little better, in some way, because I too
spent much of the day composing. Don't get me wrong; I'm
not drawing a comparison between *Simplicity* and *The Marriage
of Figaro*. It just likely assisted my transition into the character, since I knew how grueling it could be to compose original
content.

I of course worked very closely with Ian, whom I had already
known for a while. I think we originally met back in London,
when I was doing *Hair* and hanging out with the young theater
crowd. I liked him enough when we were acquaintances, though
once we started *Amadeus*, our relationship became intensely
competitive. There were some strange points of jealousy and
strain, and I suppose it's accurate to say we had quite a rivalry
while doing the play, and even a few confrontations—nothing
physical, of course. We are both very British, so any discord
between us was harmless. As a matter of fact, it ultimately provided valuable energy for the play. There was a legitimate rivalry

between Mozart and Salieri. The tension between me and Ian made sense in the wider scheme of the plot and never distorted the performance. And that's all that mattered to either of us.

Though it was nominated for a number of awards, the audience reviews of the play were mixed—in large part, I think, because Peter wrote Mozart as a deeply human, quite frail character. I had to push myself to do justice to his vision for the part. On the surface, that required that I drop about twenty pounds and develop a sort of goofy giggle. As a character, I chose to play him as being anxious and restless. Such attributes messed with the public's perception of Mozart (i.e., the more poised and elegant image of the musician on something like a chocolate box) or the figure they'd carved out based on either his music, or depictions of him in paintings. After a little more time and a few adjustments, the play eventually received acclaim and recognition, particularly for its originality and inventive portrayals. As an actor, it also gave me far greater—or at least restored—confidence in my ability to do serious stage work. Being a part of Peter's *Amadeus* felt like a real accomplishment, all the more so because it was never an easy role to play.

I loved being able to exercise several different creative muscles at once, between all of the singing and acting. I was never bored, that's for sure. But I was also playing a dangerous game in terms of setting necessary limits for myself. Recording *Simplicity* for about six hours or so during the afternoon and then doing *Amadeus* at night and preparing for film rehearsals of *Annie* to begin...well, it was unsustainable. And after what seemed like a year of twelve-hour days in three very different venues, I started feeling a desperate need to get back to England and sort of gaze at a lake and do very little at all.

Chapter Eleven

"I'll Kill Ya, Ya Little Brat. I'LL KILL YA!"

(*Annie*)

BUT I STILL HAD A MOVIE TO MAKE. WHILE LIVING IN NEW York, I'd go for the odd meeting with Ray Stark, a marvelous independent film producer. We'd often meet at the ever-bustling restaurant Sardi's, where he always ordered cinnamon toast and black coffee. I enjoyed him. At one of those meetings, when I was still performing in *Amadeus*, he brought up and then offered me the role of the wily Rooster Hannigan in the musical film version of *Annie*.

Annie originally opened on Broadway in 1977 and had received great acclaim in the years since. The musical follows the adventures of a young girl named Annie, who lives in a run-down orphanage and is later adopted by a wealthy business-man. The character I played, Rooster, is essentially a cartoon villain; he's the brother of the cruel orphanage matron, Miss Hannigan, and spends a lot of time scheming how to kidnap Annie. Not a tremendous amount of nuance to the role. He's a very cheap gangster and a rather unsuccessful one. He fancies himself a George Raft type...but he really isn't anywhere near as smooth as that. Instead, Rooster's greed and neediness are accompanied by a vicious mean streak, which is revealed by the end when he tries to kill little Annie. But he does eventually get his comeuppance after being bashed over the head by his sister, who was played by the hysterically funny, irreverent, spectacular Carol Burnett (whom I cherish).

I had great fun on the set of *Annie*, from start to finish. We started filming right around when my final album, *Simplic-ity*, came out in 1981, and it was the perfect palate cleanser, in that it was so completely different but was, in its way, another realization of a long-held dream. When I was a child, Holly-wood musicals were the only kinds of movies that my parents found suitable. For the most part, they were pretty wholesome. I particularly loved *Lili*, with Leslie Caron ("Hi-Lili, Hi-Lo"), *Seven Brides for Seven Brothers*, *Daddy Long Legs*, *South Pacific*, all of those types. I saw most several times. *Guys and Dolls* was another great one, distinguished because it spends a bit more time steeped in the gritty underworld of New York in the 1920s and 1930s.

Then there was *West Side Story*, which was in its own cat-egory, both because of the nature of the music and its sexual dynamic. Obviously, it was my favorite. I saw it in the theater in

London with George Chakiris playing Riff (odd choice, though he was marvelous) and Chita Rivera playing Anita (*always* the best choice). Seeing it on the screen, but especially seeing it live, was deeply transformative for me. I was about fifteen when I first saw it onstage, and it made me want to be a musical actor. I even stood in the rain afterward, not minding in the slightest, to get George and Chita's autographs. I immediately bought the score and learned to sing all the parts—male or female—of every tune.

Watching those Hollywood classics was my education into the sensationalism of American performed musicals. Back then, typical English musical actors didn't have a scratch on American musical actors, who were required to bring an immense amount of enthusiasm and energy to their roles. Sitting too close to the television, absorbing the song and dance and pace of those shows, it had been a (relatively) lifelong ambition to one day be on the set of a Hollywood musical—and there I was, making my mark in the film version of *Annie*.

The first order of business was to meet with the legendary John Huston, who had been tapped as the director and who needed to approve my casting as Rooster. I've had the privilege of rubbing shoulders with many great film and theater legends, but I've rarely felt awestruck. John Huston was a notable exception to that. The man was very well established for his work, of course, but he was also a rather terrifying presence. I loved him, but he could be quite alarming when he was dissatisfied. If he had a vision, he was uncompromising. If he hadn't determined what he wanted to see, he listened to his actors . . . until he wasn't interested in listening any further. He didn't suffer fools gladly, but his direction was always fair.

He was arguably a very odd choice to direct a blockbuster musical about an orphan charming her way to luxury, but I think they chose him because he knew the period, having lived through it. Plus, he was probably up for a challenge (and for the paycheck).

I went to his hotel, the Sherry-Netherland, to have a drink with him and discuss Rooster and make sure he found me tolerable. In his deep, touchstone croaky voice, he asked, "So...what ideas do you have about the part?"

"Well, I thought I would show up," I replied.

He chortled with surprise and some type of amusement. I had just wrapped up a play on Broadway and let him know I'd been closely watching a stagehand who fidgeted a lot, in a very New Jersey sort of way. Whenever I'm looking to develop details for any given character, I've often found it helpful to observe people around me and listen closely, to understand how they live in the world. Just as that older woman on the bus had inspired the way Dr. Frank-N-Furter speaks, this stagehand's jitters animated Rooster's physical character. I'd highly recommend the practice to any aspiring actor. Just watch people, especially those whose mannerisms are foreign to you. Much inspiration is afforded to us by paying attention to others, and then imitating them.

I did a brief example for Huston of this stagehand's tone and physical demeanor—though it was the latter that really distinguished him.

"Yes, yes. Very good. Yes, that's right on the money," he said in his inimitable gravelly voice. He followed up with: "Do you want to talk about it?"

"Well...not really," I said.

"Oh! Well. Thank *Gaaawd*. A lot of actors like to talk. I listen, but it's exhausting. If you don't need to, that's fine. Just fine. Very good."

That was the extent of our introduction and preparation. John was confident, and I was too at that point. I had been chosen among some serious contenders for the role, and my castmates were all incredibly talented.

I know John has a mixed reputation, but I don't really give a toss about that. I really came to love and respect him. He didn't direct me much, because I simply didn't make many appearances in the film. But when he did, it was obvious that he knew exactly what he was doing. He never said "Cut" until we had gotten a shot exactly right. It's extraordinary to have that kind of trust in your director, and for him to be so very decisive. He also left a great deal of room for us to grow into our characters within the frame of his broad vision.

The best part of making *Annie*, however, was the amount of fun I had with my costars, particularly Carol and Bernadette Peters, who played my love interest/co-swindler, Lily St. Regis. It was a riot. There was not a comment I could make that Carol wouldn't elevate to the next absurd level with a retort that would either challenge me or just leave me in stitches. And Bernadette could keep up, too—she was dating Steve Martin and had just as quick a wit about her. Between the two of them, I spent six weeks straight laughing for hours a day.

We had a real banger of a time for our number "Easy Street." We did two very distinct versions of it. The original was shot out on the street, with something like one hundred dancers lined up

behind the three of us (Carol, Bernadette, and me). There may
have been more. There were people dancing on air-conditioning
units, and also a little robbery happening on a fire escape
nearby; John was great, and very particular, at getting right
those kinds of small human performances. The result was basically a well-choreographed circus spectacle. But after the whole
editing process, it was deemed to be over the top, which was
fair enough. After all, it didn't communicate "Easy Street," and
those in charge already knew that the film would be criticized
as being overproduced.

We were brought back about a month later to reshoot a jubi-
lant, swanky version of the song with just the three of us at the
orphanage. We had such fantastic harmony, so knew we could
pull it off. Thankfully, there was a stunt double for me, who
performed all kinds of gymnastics and acrobatic feats, namely
my slide down the banister of the stairs. I've always wanted to
thank whoever it was. Sadly, I can't recall his name and didn't
engage with him much. I trust he was happy enough, and the
movement was executed with a kind of grace and ease I never
could have matched. But if you're out there reading this, and
you once slid down a banister backward in my place, I would
like to take this moment to officially let you know how grateful
I am for your service.

Though it was a bit of a pain to completely redo a whole song
and dance number, my respect for Huston held strong. I especially appreciated the extent to which he would just let us get
on with it. He was a part of every shot that we filmed, but he
wasn't hugely hands-on, and as long as we nailed the shot, he
wasn't terribly precious about how we got there.

The choreographer, Joe Layton, was very hands-on. He had to be. He was actually our replacement choreographer; he'd been hired after they decided that the first take of "Easy Street" was a bust. I'd seen some of his work before—he'd directed Bette Midler in her *Clams on the Half Shell Revue*—and I was grateful to be in such good hands, especially since *Annie* was exceptionally strenuous. I did more physical work (of a very different variety than what I'd expended for *Rocky Horror*) than I had ever done before. It wasn't just the dancing—it was jumping over fences, being in chase scenes, climbing bridges. I had never trained properly for that kind of movement and coordination, and I'm no Steve McQueen. But thankfully, everybody was very patient with me, and—again, thanks to my costars—we laughed our way through it.

Shot in both Hollywood and New Jersey, the whole atmosphere of the set for *Annie* was notably different from my previous projects. Despite the enormous budget and high-profile cast, there wasn't the pressure I'd felt with other productions, even though I found the choreography challenging. I think it was largely due to the environment John cultivated on set; he simply loved filmmaking, as did the cast and crew, and this meant we could enjoy ourselves in the process of making something instead of worrying excessively over how it was going to turn out.

In addition to John's influence and the fabulous chemistry with my scene partners, we also had an all-star crew supporting us and enhancing the film. (Thankfully, I didn't have many scenes with the titular orphan herself. I'm sure that Aileen Quinn was a lovely young girl, but as the old adage goes, one

tries to avoid working with children or animals. *Annie* had both.)
I had the privilege of working out my costumes with the legendary Theoni Aldredge, who won a bunch of much-deserved
Tonys and Oscars for her work. Boy, did she know what she was
doing. Most of my clothes were made just for me, including the
shoes—which felt very glamorous.

I'll never be able to say enough about working with Carol.
There's just nobody like Carol Burnett, nobody in the world.
We had such a ball playing off each other. She is just such a
solid human, and naturally hysterical. While we were filming,
she used to host these dinners at her house, and her sister, who
lived with her, cooked these marvelous meals for us. Then afterward, we'd all play charades, which was Carol's idea of a good
time—mine, too, when you're playing with Carol and Bernadette and Steve Martin.

When we wrapped, I asked her, "What's up next? What are
you going to do now?" She had played a much more central
role, as the villainous Miss Hannigan, so she'd been in for a
more exhausting haul. She simply dropped one of her smiles at
me and drawled, "Honey, I'm going to go home to Hawaii and
watch the whales fucking."

I laughed so hard I couldn't stand upright.

Alas, I would not be joining her, nor going home to Hawaii.
However, in rare moments of quiet, I still couldn't shake the
feeling that my time in New York had expired. I longed for a
spell back home. All in, my itchy feet were delighted to carry
me back to England.

Chapter Twelve

London Lights and Lows

ITCHY FEET OR NOT, I'M A CHOREOGRAPHER'S NIGHTMARE. Over the course of my career, I've often begged or even paid dance captains to stay during lunchtime to help my feet memorize the steps. Luckily, they've tended to be very generous about that. I can be quite good at dancing when taught, but it's just not the type of movement that comes naturally to me. The most helpful choreographers are the ones who have taken the time and bothered to learn the way my body moves. From that point, they can do quite a bit with me. But I need that kind of help to show me precisely where the weight and emphasis of each step and gesture should be. Otherwise, I'm lost. A devoted choreographer can make all the difference.

I was blessed with one for my next major stage performance, a pop revival of *The Pirates of Penzance*. The production's wonderful choreographer, Graciela Daniele, was a Brazilian woman, and as far as I was concerned, essentially directed the play. She was the heart and soul of it, and I was very lucky indeed because we got on marvelously. We rehearsed my introductory song, "I Am a Pirate King" (*and it is, it is a glorious thing to be a Pirate King*), countless times, but I couldn't get it quite right.

Graciela observed me closely for a while and we tried out a few methods, none of which broke through. Finally, she gave me a playful look and directed me to "do it like Chita." I laughed and nodded, then did my best to channel the spirit and attack of Chita Rivera, which proved to be the key to my whole performance.

She got it; she really did. She understood that something was holding me back, and then unlocked it by telling me to put some fucking attitude into it. That, I could manage.

I'd first been asked to do *The Pirates of Penzance* while I still lived in New York, but I turned down the role because I didn't appreciate the concept of making a more modern version of the original, a comic opera by Gilbert and Sullivan that follows Frederic, a young apprentice mistakenly bound to a band of tenderhearted pirates, led by the Pirate King. I felt protective of its tradition and its period (don't worry, I acknowledge as much with a healthy eye roll). But I was also still working on *Amadeus* at the time, and it felt too much in conflict with that responsibility.

When I saw the show, Kevin Kline was playing the role of the Pirate King, and he was absolutely brilliant. I so admired the way he was carrying the part and the play that it filled me with a bit of remorse. "That would be great fun to be a part of," I thought.

I was friendly with Kevin, so after the show, I went backstage to see him and asked him how he was coping with the role, if it had been a big burden. Kevin used to turn down so much work that producers called him "Kevin Decline," so I knew if he had agreed to take on the part, that really said something. Anyways, I let him know that he had been so dynamic that he'd made me reconsider my decision not to play it. I don't know whether he communicated as much to the director, but when they decided to do it in London, just as I was moving back, I was offered the role again.

That time, however, I replied with a grateful and resounding "Yes."

———

We opened at Drury Lane in May of 1982. Playing the Pirate King was a refreshing change and a gift, not merely because I was back in London, or because I was encouraged to flaunt my moves by releasing my inner Chita, but also because I received my first official singing lessons since my schooling at Kingswood. In New York, they'd hired a wonderful vocal coach for Linda Ronstadt, who'd played Mabel in the show and had to be trained to hit some of the more difficult notes. They brought the same coach over to London, to my great fortune.

In some ways, it felt bizarre, because the show didn't come long after the end of my rock 'n' roll career and suddenly I was taking singing lessons. However, playing the Pirate King was very vocally demanding, and included a couple of high notes that I had determined were simply outside of my range.

One day, after listening to me sing and patiently enduring my insistent claims that we would have to change the key because I didn't have a falsetto, the vocal coach told me: "Nonsense. *Everyone* has a falsetto."

I kept resisting, but she was determined to find one in my range. A little while later, she had an evident revelation.

"Were you ever a boy soprano?" she asked.

When I told her that I had been, her eyes brightened. She nodded knowingly.

"I know why you can't reach it. You're in mourning for the sound you made as a boy."

I'm not sure why that specific bit of feedback has remained with me for all the decades since. It struck me as an extraordinary idea—that my voice would be inhibited due to grieving the pureness of what it once was. I immediately realized that she was right, and not long after, I recovered my falsetto. I'd have *never* hit all my notes without being able to access that. Interestingly enough, that falsetto swiftly disappeared again shortly after my stint as the Pirate King. I've never found it since—nor have I sought it out.

So, I learned to dance with high-octane attitude, I relearned how to sing like a schoolboy, and as a result, I was finally able to make my mum proud of what I was doing... or at least relatively pleased in how my career might benefit her.

In general, my mother was unimpressed (at best) and even embarrassed by any success I may have had. But she did like it when it enabled her to meet royalty. *Pirates of Penzance* was doing very well in London and was successful enough to bring in the Queen Mother on her eightieth birthday. She sat in the royal box and the entire audience sang "Happy Birthday" to her, I think during the intermission. Once everybody had cleared out, she was brought down to the stage to meet the cast and I presented her with an enormous cake.

We were all aware that this would be happening... as was my mother, who made a rare showing at one of my performances and muscled her way through the stage door and into the wings to be in proximity to the Queen Mother.

I wheeled this colossal-sized cake onstage for Her Majesty to cut, but they had neglected to provide me with a proper knife— they had just given me this sort of measly slicer. We both stared at the cake, then the Queen Mother offered me one of her thousand-watt smiles. "I think perhaps we ought to try your trusty sword," she said, looking pointedly at the huge pirate weapon slung around my waist. Luckily, somebody had rushed on with an actual knife by that point. We both laughed, and I so respected her generous energy. Plus, you could really sense that she had a fun spirit. And it was nice that my mother got to see me in *something*, no matter the underlying reason for her interest.

The Pirate King was a blast as an out-front role of a big musical, and I was delighted to be performing on the London stage again after what felt like a long time away. It's not like there was some grand homecoming woven into the experience. They still didn't quite know what to make of me in London in acting circles, really. They weren't sure (or didn't care) what I could do. But I didn't feel like a foreigner for once, and I loved being home. I relished having old friends and old haunts to visit, a fun play in a legendary theater (with an extraordinary dressing room), and just the familiarity of London.

Playing the Pirate King night after night, however, was supremely exhausting. It's a role that requires enormous stores of energy. Not only is the choreography pretty athletic, but to pull off the part, you have to be full-out for two and a half hours, night after night. I mean, the kind of force of personality that would be impossible to maintain in my personal life. I've never met anybody who could maintain that force onstage *and* in their day-to-day. Those who attempt as much will almost certainly burn out very early on. So even though it was a very lively time professionally, I kept a much quieter social life than I had been maintaining in New York—which was probably for the best.

———

Shortly after that *Pirates of Penzance* run, I fell backward into a nonstop routine at the Royal National Theatre, which I joined primarily because I longed to return to the world of words and the delight of performing them in front of an audience. Once there, I performed in plays like *The Rivals*, *Love for Love*, and *The Threepenny Opera*—all directed by my old friend Peter Wood. Being reunited with him was great, but the stretch at the National was exhilarating, then rather exhausting.

There were several plays on rotation at the National. We performed *Love for Love*, an eighteenth-century comedy by Sheridan that satirizes love, marriage, and greed through a mess of romantic entanglements scheming for fortune and affection. We put it on as part of British Week in Vienna. I'm not sure what the thinking was behind all of that; I presume it was some sort of awful promotional deal.

By a strange coincidence (considering the plot of our play), Charles and Diana were also in attendance, representing England. At the end of the show, we went up into the corridor where the royal box was, and the cast lined up so that the Crown Prince and Princess could meet us. Diana looked beautiful and was very natural. When meeting the Royals, one usually expects a great deal of formality, but Diana broke the ice immediately. She had on a blue sequin dress, but a few of the sequins had fallen off.

"Is there anyone here from wardrobe?" she asked, smiling flirtatiously with all of us. "I've left a trail of sequins from the royal box." She was quite charming, amusing, and comfortable in her own skin.

They proceeded to meet with everyone from the cast in line. When she reached me, she paused and said, "You were in the *Rocky Horror Show*, weren't you?"

"Yes, ma'am. I...don't suppose you saw it," I said.

"Of course I saw it," she continued, then waited a beat before giving me a little cheeky grin. "It quite completed my education!"

I found it a wonderfully royal thing to say. It's challenging to describe how simultaneously stately and sweet she was. I liked her instantly. She moved on, and I was then introduced to Charles. (I can't get used to calling him King Charles, and don't imagine I ever will—I find it terribly strange that he's on the currency.) It wasn't the first time I had encountered him; I used to catch glimpses of him from time to time in Cambridge, whenever I would go visit Richard. Charles would ride his bicycle around the streets and blush a deep tomato red whenever he made eye contact with... *anybody*. He seemed so very nervous. It was rather sweet, really.

Anyway, on the evening when we were formally introduced, he shuffled in beside Diana and said, rather awkwardly, "Erm. I think I've seen you on television."

"Well spotted, sir," I replied.

During that period, he might have been referring to any number of television productions on which I was working (the Royals do *love* their television shows). Playing Bill Sikes in *Oliver Twist*, a book I had loved as a boy, stands out for me. I feel sorry for villains from bygone times, when people had so little room to be different. There are still lots of Fagins and Sikeses around, but they'll be fine.

I spent most of my time on the stage, however, with *The Pirates of Penzance* remaining in my memory as the bright spot, where I had the most amount of fun and felt I was thriving in the role in which I was cast.

But I was by no means delighted by everything we put on at the National. Seared most painfully into that run was the darker challenge I had playing Macheath (or Mack the Knife) in *The Threepenny Opera*. My performance was not an unqualified success. Truth be told, that one was a bit of a nightmare. It turned out to be among my most insurmountable roles, which made me very unhappy. No matter how hard I tried, I just couldn't bring it off. I had the flash and dazzle to play the character; I knew that. But I didn't have sufficient gravity or the authority necessary to really capture him.

There are a lot of group scenes with his gang in *The Threepenny Opera*. And to play him properly, it's important that Mack dominates the crew—and that the audience knows it. But I just wasn't sure how to do so. Looking back, I think I put too much reliance on the dialogue, hoping the words would be able to elevate the character. But it didn't feel authentic to me to step into his shoes... and that lack of authenticity was reflected in the performance. It always felt like I was faking it.

When I first started playing him—and it was for a good amount of time; around two years or so, several nights a week—I originally carried him as a sort of Michael Caine type. But then I got fed up with that voice, so I brought his tone down a bit to more of a gravelly Sean Connery tone. That worked better, because it evoked a tougher character.

In retrospect, of course, it's easy for me to acknowledge now that it wasn't yet the time for me to play that character. I'd hoped that having Peter as the director would help, but he was only really the director in a hands-off, nominal sense. He didn't bother with the production as much as I would have liked, nor did he take the time to discuss how I might be able to evolve into the role. I don't quite know why, but it made me feel awfully depressed.

Mack must carry great confidence onto the stage. That wasn't a problem. But in Mack's case, it should be a confidence afforded by age as well as achievement. By this point, I was only in my forties, and I strongly feel you should be closer to your sixties to carry off the role as it's intended. I suppose it would be a bit like casting a younger actor as King Lear. My depression around the whole thing manifested itself as a kind of idle sadness, one that kept me from rectifying the situation. I had people I could have talked to about it, but I didn't bother. I've always preferred to get on with things on my own when possible.

———

Shortly afterward, I was cast in a feature film called *The Ploughman's Lunch*, which was really what broke me out of the funk I had been in about *The Threepenny Opera*. It was an unlikely release, as I played a totally urbane Englishman. It's always refreshing to get a break from the larger-than-life characters that I was often cast as. Written by Ian McEwan, it takes place in the aftermath of the Falklands War. It's very witty and rather talky, born out of the progressive politics of the time and meant to address the mass media's fixation on Margaret Thatcher. Jonathan Pryce and Rosemary Harris were the costars. I don't recall a great deal from the performance, just that I loved doing it and that it wasn't wildly successful, but that didn't matter to me. For one scene, we went to the Conservative Party Conference to shoot, and just by great chance were there on a day when we managed to get Thatcher live on film, simply by showing up. That was a huge stroke of luck. I say luck, but we all hated her.

Other than that notable exception, I largely enjoyed performing with the National, but I had gotten my fill of words and of less expected roles, and my pantry and paychecks reflected the extent to which I was not exactly performing on the West End. Ever the vagabond, I also knew there were new roads and worlds of opportunity back in the States, and I was ready to mix it up a bit. A few months prior to leaving, I started longing for the freshness of a different locale. I was also eager to get back to a larger film production, which would mean returning to America. I felt ready. Though, thinking back on it now, I wasn't entirely prepared for the demands of the roles ahead.

After all, how *do* you prepare to play the devil?

Chapter Thirteen

"What Is Light Without Dark?"

(*Legend*)

WICKEDNESS, IT SEEMS, COMES NATURALLY TO ME. OR, AT least, others evidently see it as a trait I'm capable of accessing and reflecting in front of an audience. This was made most obvious when I returned to America and, within a very short span of time, was cast to take on the roles of the Lord of Darkness in the film *Legend* and Pennywise the Clown in the TV film *It*. There were characters I played between the two, thank God. But similar tactics were employed to help me understand and bring to life the inherent evil of those roles.

People often ask me if I have a certain preference or fondness for playing villains, and my go-to response has always been that villains are better written than heroes, which I still believe to be true. They're less predictable. There's more variety. They're also fun to escape into, they command attention, and audiences find them fascinating, even liberating.

Much as I enjoy trampling about in the dark arts through these characters, I also like to add in a bit of my own mischief, where there's room, so that my characters are both enjoyable to watch and enjoyable to play. I like the notion of playing somebody who is so frightening that you can't bear to look but *also* can't bear to look away.

So, where's the limit? I don't think there is one. Or at least I've never encountered a character who felt too dark to take on. If there had been one, that probably would have intrigued me enough that I would want to play him anyway. I did eventually play a serial killer named Billy Flynn on the TV show *Criminal Minds*, which I found altogether more difficult and darker than Darkness or Pennywise because of the fact that beneath the monster, he was oh so very human. But very few parts are cruel beyond redemption. Or so cruel as to not be touched by glimmers of light and playfulness.

The thing is, I don't truly believe in irredeemably dark people.

Around the time that I was in *The Pirates of Penzance*, so the early to mid-eighties, Ridley Scott started putting together the cast for his big film *Legend*. It was Ridley's go at creating a world of pure fantasy. Darkness, which is the part I would play, seeks to create eternal night by destroying the last of the unicorns. (Yes, it's that level of fantasy.) The sprightly young bright-eyed Jack, who was played by Tom Cruise, teams up with a group to save the world and Princess Lili (played by Mia Sara) from me, despite the great power that I wield.

I suppose it's a compliment, albeit a slightly alarming one, when a big-time director is considering "Who should play the devil?" and your name instantly springs to mind as being a natural for the role.

In fairness, that wasn't *precisely* how I came to land it.

Ridley later told me that when he was looking for someone to play the Lord of Darkness, he screened a lot of films—including *The Rocky Horror Picture Show*, to consider Richard O'Brien as a possible candidate for the role. After watching it, however, he decided I might be a better fit. He wanted somebody larger than life, and while I know Richard would have loved to have been cast as the Lord of Darkness, if you're looking for power and dominance, that wouldn't have been obvious from observing his character in *Rocky Horror*. I think Ridley also recognized, while watching it, that I wasn't afraid to take risks with my performances—as long as and especially if they were true to the characters I was playing.

I had never worked with somebody like Ridley. He really is spectacular when it comes to advanced visuals and production, and he deserves all accolades for what he's created—from *Alien* to *Blade Runner* to *Gladiator*. But initially, he gets less involved in the acting and performance execution. At least that was the case when we started filming. The hands-off approach was a new experience for me in terms of film, and required a lot of adjustment, as my interpretation of a role had always depended first on the words, then on the director. Increasing numbers of directors, particularly of films that demand attention to special effects and so on, don't seem to get as involved in the acting, which is a shame. With all the best directors, in my experience, you work on and work out a character pretty much between the two of you—at least at the start—then the role grows from that mutual understanding of who you're trying to embody.

When directors opt for highly produced, visually ambitious films, they have to consider a lot more details and handle other pressing matters that are often more complicated—or at the very least consuming—than the acting. There was no time to create such an elaborate fantasy world, like the set of *Legend* truly was, and then also sit down with the cast and talk to them about their characters' motivation or whatever. As a result, I had to be more thoughtful about measuring my own performance and deciding what it was that I wanted to do with the role.

I've always been very critical of my own performances. Not consistently, but often enough. It's like any other part of being a human: There are times when you like yourself better than at other moments. I've spent much of my life unable to watch myself on the screen. I'm better about that now, but I've been afforded plenty of time to get over it. For example, back when we started working on *Legend*, I would have never gone to rushes. Rushes are basically clips of the day's work that get played the next morning so the crew can figure out what needs to be adjusted, if anything, before the film is too close to being finished to do anything about it. They're mostly for the benefit of technical departments, like lighting and sound, and I guess makeup and hair, to assess how everybody looks in celluloid and whatnot. Actors tend to get in the way, because they focus more on their impact on the screen, rather than the screen's impact on them. But I remember being asked if I wanted to attend and I resolutely refused.

The process of becoming that beast was a horrifically claustrophobic glimpse of hell…which I suppose wasn't *entirely* inappropriate, given my character. The physical characterization of Darkness was based on William Blake's painting entitled *The Ghost of a Flea*, which features a hunchback figure with a bulbous head. To this framework, Ridley and Rob Bottin (the extremely talented primary prosthetic and makeup artist) added the body of a minotaur, because…why not? We went through several stages of experimentation, as Darkness originally had a much more wolflike face with very serious teeth that would have made it impossible for me to speak.

They eventually decided on a physical appearance of evil that included truly massive horns and hooves, but it was all built upon my human form. I had no part in making that decision. I was just informed that to embody this larger-than-life character, my entire body would be significantly enhanced and sculpted, which was achieved by adding prosthetic bulk.

The men who designed and constructed the prosthetics for *Legend* have a huge, peculiar, gritty workshop in Monrovia, where I was sent to have my casts fitted to me, bits at a time— which was damn uncomfortable. It is beyond strange to have a mold made of your entire body. I don't recommend it. The first fitting was particularly important, and required me to be there for something like twelve hours total. This was not a fitting for a costume; this was a fitting of the kind of full-body plaster I would have to wear if I had broken every bone in my body. At the time, it seemed a little slapdash. They placed bandages all over my body before applying the plaster, which then set like rock while I waited for *ten hours.*

At that initial fitting, I was instructed not to take a deep breath. That became particularly unfortunate after several hours, when I began to feel a rising wave of panic and utter claustrophobia. Remember: this was the mid-eighties, and helpful sedatives like Xanax or Valium weren't quite the readily available supplements they might be in such a setting today. I knew I needed to be relatively still, but when that anxiety began rearing up, they had nothing on hand to settle me down. I was also sitting in a bathtub—they couldn't simply rip it off and let me breathe; I had to sit in a bath for roughly an hour to liquefy the soluble gum used to create the human body cast—which somewhat limited our options. In any event, they agreed to pour wine into my mouth in a last-ditch attempt to try to keep me calm. It did not serve that purpose.

After sitting for over ten hours, I'd had enough and just ripped part of the plaster off, but in doing so, I also ripped some of the glue that was stuck to my skin. I suppose I learned my lesson (indescribable pain will do that to a person) and tried to remain calm as I stood there, propped up, while they cut me out of the rest of it with circular saws—the real ones they use for any plaster cast. They had to go down my entire body, and I knew that if I failed to keep absolutely still…well, I didn't know what would happen, which in and of itself undoubtedly took a few years off of my life. It was a horror scene, for all of us.

Fortunately for everyone involved, the end result (of the prosthetics, not of the wine nor the saw) was an inarguably masterful work of craftsmanship, especially for the time. Bottin was nominated for an Academy Award for the effects he created for *Legend*. These were extraordinarily clever artists, and I have great awe and respect for what they managed to pull off, especially given that I was far from the most patient or serene model.

Once they had the basic cast, they had to surgically glue my whole "body" together each day from about three different pieces before beginning on the makeup. The whole process of turning me into the Lord of Darkness took roughly six hours, every day of filming. That was a whole lot of work for them, not to mention incredibly tedious for me to sit there being made into an enhanced, satanic version of myself. But I was committed. And it probably prepared me well to rule mightily and impatiently over the dominion of hell. I was grateful that people from the cast and crew were very kind, or curious, and little groups would come in and chat with me as I was being transformed.

While shooting *Legend*, my routine, more or less, required that I arrive at 6:30 in the morning, then the team would get to work on me. At 12:30, everyone would break for lunch, and then I would go to the set and be the first shot afterward. We would shoot until maybe 7:00 or 8:00 at night, when I would return to be released from the prosthetic prison. Once we got into a rhythm, we could remove the whole thing in about an hour and a half—in a bizarre process that involved ripping it open at the top and pouring in solvent while I was sitting in a hot bath.

It was very peculiar to embody a character for several hours and then feel like I was being opened up like a can and gradually peeled away at, piece by piece. The first time they removed it, the prosthetics were just ripped off (as I had done when it was being set), which left my body covered with blisters. It was so bad that after leaving, I drove immediately to a hospital to have my body medically photographed as a precaution, just in case I would need to file a suit later on.

The hooves were a whole other element of the spectacle. They were something like a foot tall, so I had to practice walking on them like stilts. I found I could walk up a flight of stairs but curiously, and somewhat problematically, not down. From the hooves to the top of my horns, I stood at 8'1", which is a pretty wild feeling when you're used to being about 5'9" (when I'm in my boots). The horns were colossal. For a few of the scenes, my movements were so extensive that they required a type of harness to keep them strapped to my head—less because of their weight (they were remarkably light) and more because of their enormity.

Imagine being physically elevated more than two feet, walking around set with many pounds worth of prosthetics. People treat you differently.

But that may have been because I looked like Satan, sounded like Satan, and had the eyes of an evil cat. Hard to say.

————

Those latter elements required some highly unusual, bizarre negotiations. Ironically, after all those hours of additions and enhancements, as an actor I was reduced to little other than my voice. I didn't even have my own eyes; instead, I had to wear these huge contact lenses that covered my eyes and turned them into vertical slits. This involved yet another very painful process that originally included pouring plastic molding material into my eye and grinding the lenses until they fit; unsurprisingly, it was very uncomfortable. I protested needing the lenses at first, but then I saw what I looked like with them in. It was pretty extraordinary. I was totally unrecognizable to myself, but I looked incredible.

I still fought with Ridley to let me use my own voice, as opposed to what he had in mind for the sound of Darkness.

"Guys, since the only thing left of me is my voice, could I please use it?" was among one of the more surreal pleas that I heard myself utter. After not a small amount of back-and-forth, he agreed to give me that. And I was very lucky, because my voice still leaves me with a lot to work with. In the end, Ridley got his way, too; in post-production, they made my voice even deeper and added a bit of echo and reverb in order to make my character sound as sinister as possible.

Were there any perks to wearing a full-body cast, balancing on mini-stilt hooves, while still trying to embody control, power, and dominance? Of course! Memorably, Grace Jones—who was filming the James Bond movie *A View to a Kill* on the same lot, maybe even in the next studio—used to come in and visit with me, primarily because she loved my peculiar gear. While I was getting it applied, she would often muse about having one or two prosthetic devices made for herself. She enjoyed taking a lot of very funny Polaroids of the two of us as I was midway through the infernal process. She was particularly fascinated by my face. She longed to wear it, really; she'd always stroke it, almost tenderly, as though I wasn't even present beneath it all. It was quite strange. But she was entirely her own person: incredibly entertaining, astonishingly beautiful, quite mad, and fully in control of—and unafraid to use—her power. I always very much looked forward to her company, and my terrifying face helped to keep bringing her back.

The prosthetics and makeup, though, were just the pre-party. Going out and acting after that was a whole other adventure. I didn't have to do much theatrical digging in order to play Darkness. I just showed up. How would one research the devil, anyway? Going to Vegas, perhaps—a place I loathe. I find casinos to be sad temples to vulgarity, really.

As for my costar? I didn't really engage with Tom Cruise all that much, perhaps because this wasn't the type of film where we'd all sit around chatting—Ridley didn't foster that environment, and in my case my prosthetics regimen meant I couldn't exactly go out for pints prior to having my horns and hooves removed. By the end of my extrication I would be ready for nowhere but my own bed.

Before we met on the set of *Legend*, I had seen *Risky Business*, with Tom cast perfectly as the cute, innocent young rebel. And when we finally appeared in a film together, he was very nice and easy to be around—but he's also quite unique, and not a person I fully understood. We never had any issues, but I cannot say I felt the appeal. Unlike many others in the eighties, I wasn't desperately starstruck around him; in fact, I was kind of dreading it. I couldn't really identify why. Maybe he sensed my reticence and was consequently a little awkward. He was very into fully embodying his role, and I believe even requested to sleep on the snow set because he wanted to feel at home there. In the premise of the film, he loses his power, but he looks great doing it. He has the perks that looks and money bring in Hollywood. I mean, people all over the world want to fuck him—and I'm sure that wouldn't be the worst feeling. I was just never blown away by his talent. Then again, my senses were no doubt dulled beneath my prosthetics.

There's not much I can say definitively about him, since we didn't get to know each other very well, but at the end of the day I found him to be a very thoughtful, considerate colleague— which I appreciated.

———

The most interesting challenge of the movie, and the one that came to intrigue me, was trying to figure out how to give this terrifying creature—who appeared to have punched his way through a comic book—authentic qualities, how to project something human through all that plaster and plastic. And that experiment became my primary motivation.

It required compassion and a very healthy dose of my dad's universal empathy to find a connection with a character who is defined by his cruelty, vindictiveness, and ostentatiously hideous appearance. But I certainly tried and, hopefully in somebody's eyes, succeeded in complicating and animating Darkness by giving him moments that resembled a charm he couldn't stifle, and a capacity for seduction that is no doubt predatory but also rooted in a desire for companionship. He also has a rather evident libido, of which he's unafraid. I did find a connection eventually and am most grateful that Ridley sought me out for the role.

Ultimately, though nobody is asking me for my verdict, I think *Legend* had the same primary flaw that *Blade Runner* did—and I absolutely love *Blade Runner*. In both films, Ridley (at times) was so obsessed with a dynamic visual that he didn't always have his eye on keeping the narrative together. Of course, most viewers don't mind! These films do look quite literally spectacular and are very ahead of their time. Still, the stories drag and it's easy to get a bit lost.

Ridley will always use the take where the light hits the pillar at the ideal moment visually, no matter what's happening with the actors. So you quickly learn that whenever you're on his set, you need to just keep doing whatever you're doing until that moment hits.

Which is not in any way to suggest that he's not a good man. He is incredibly generous with his actors and lets us contribute our thoughts to how any given frame gets shot. He asks your opinion and, notably, he listens to your reply and actually takes it into consideration. I appreciate how much he values his actors' perspectives, which he doesn't necessarily need to do, and isn't always the case.

With all that noted, my memories of the film have always been consumed by the challenges of my demonic armor. I almost never discuss the character of Darkness, just the effects. Or, of course, the devastating fire that ravaged the entire set of *Legend*, which was a sort of fantastical forest, as well as the Bond stage beside it. That was horrendous. It didn't help that Pinewood Studios, where we shot the film, was filled with highly flammable Styrofoam snow that went up in sheets of flames in a matter of minutes. Ridley was very calm about the whole thing, and really took it in stride. In fact, I believe he got the news and then immediately went to play tennis. They rebuilt the set entirely, which was damn impressive, and in what felt like no time at all, we proceeded with the filming.

Naturally, my mother assumed that I must have been smoking. In her mind, there was no doubt that my cigarette butts caused the legendary fire.

Chapter Fourteen

"I Buttle, Sir"

(*Clue*)

THE ROLES I WAS PRIVILEGED TO PLAY WITHIN A ROUGHLY six-year stretch certainly tested my range. Leaping from Rooster to Mozart to the Pirate King to Darkness, and then on to Wadsworth and Pennywise, demanded that I stretch in every direction as an actor—and I loved that varied, uphill climb.

Clue, the film rendering of the well-known board game, was naturally a highlight. *Clue* was the brainchild of a group of young moguls, including John Landis, who'd been deputized to direct it. He wrestled with the script for a while before handing off the writing to Jonathan Lynn. Lynn was riding high on the success of a very popular British sitcom called

Yes Minister, which highlighted the absurdity of ministerial bureaucracy. I don't think he'd ever directed a film before, but after he nailed down the script, Landis and the other moguls signed off on him directing it.

When the part of Wadsworth, the dutiful and slightly smarmy butler, came to me out of the blue, I jumped at the opportunity. Jonny and I had known each other for a very long time, having gone to boarding school together. I had revered him as a remarkable young actor—he was sort of my hero back in my teenage years. But he was a few years older so we had never been in a production together, though I wish we had been. Knowing him in that light, I was particularly impressed when I first read his script for an ambitious film based on the game. The writing is sharp, fast-paced, and utterly brilliant, which is all the more impressive because it also has to be so compact.

That's not to say I wasn't intimidated. In candor, I was appalled by the demands of the script, particularly when it became clear that my character would go through long stretches without ever really drawing a breath. Because of that, I approached the role like I would for a part in a play, where you memorize the whole thing in one go. When I first received the script, I was staying at the Bel-Air hotel and was about twenty pounds heavier than I wanted to be for the camera, so I rented a stationary bike and used to exercise in my room while learning my lines and waiting to meet the rest of the cast. It felt much more manageable when I realized I'd only be shooting three to four pages of script a day; back then, my short-term memory was rather good.

Perhaps because it was his first film, or because the script was so demanding, Jonny set up rehearsals and we had this big room in the studio at Paramount. We didn't rehearse the whole thing, but we did go over most of it. Jonny was very concerned with the pacing of the film; he wanted it to be like those classic movies from the forties, like *His Girl Friday*. Since *Clue* is both a spoof *and* a whodunit, the dialogue needs to run at that same kind of breakneck speed in order to really work. I thought it was very appropriate and exciting as an actor. Rehearsals were also very reassuring because we had such a good cast, with people like Madeline Kahn (who's something of a genius and plays the black widow, Mrs. White), Michael McKean (a more low-key actor who kept the character of Mr. Green, a state department employee, rather grounded), and Eileen Brennan (as Mrs. Peacock, the senator's wife, who had the most extraordinary drawl and played the part with a great deal of energy).

I loved getting the chance to work alongside these actors; we had great fun and grew to really care for one another. When she found out I was staying in a hotel, Madeline was shocked.

"Oh, Tim, come on," she said. "You don't want to stay in a hotel. I have a friend who's got a very nice house in the hills that you should rent."

I was eager to see it, so we went together and it was very nice indeed. Originally built by John Barrymore, it was Tudor-ish, with a U shape around the pool and an amazing view of Los Angeles and the Valley. I later learned it had also been the site of an infamous and rather morbid party; after he died, some of John's friends snuck his body out of the morgue and drove it to a sort of "final farewell" at the house, where he was propped up at the dining room table. I can't say any of our parties were quite as rousing, but it was a fun bit of trivia all the same.

My friend June Roberts, with whom I had been flatmates in London very early in our careers, happened to also be in town,

writing a funny screenplay for Cher called *Mermaids*. I invited
her to join me in the house while she finished up the writing.
She was a riot, albeit quite reactive and highly unpredictable.
One day, she got so frustrated by writer's block that she stood
up, sighed dramatically, and then threw her typewriter into the
pool.

We entertained regularly—Sunday brunches, mainly, because
I was working so hard on the film. That was a very good time
in my life. I liked where I was living, I had great friends around
me, and I was genuinely enjoying the role I was playing, however draining it felt at times.

———

My connection to Wadsworth primarily lies in his sincere feeling for service. He's a curious man who takes very seriously his
role of delivering as elegantly as possible. To buttle *as elegantly
as possible*. It was great fun to combine that quality with his limited respect for the other characters in the movie. Butlers almost
always behave as though the house belongs to them. They carry
an arrogance that they're not quite entitled to have, and I loved
playing around with those qualities. I was also given a lot of
support and freedom to do so.

Though the studio originally tossed around the ideas of John
Cleese, Leonard Rossiter, or Rowan Atkinson playing the butler, Jonny went out of his way to insist that I would be an ideal
Wadsworth, and one who had sufficient stateside recognition.
Jonny's faith in me gave me extra incentive to do right by both
him and the film. Given the character, the writing, and the pacing, I always had to be quite disciplined, even when the rest of
the cast were frolicking about between takes. And if any film

rivaled *Annie* for physical exertion, it would certainly have been *Clue*. After all, Wadsworth spends much of the third act running around demonstrating how each potential murder took place—and all with brisk, proper timing.

We spent an intense few weeks together as cast and crew, going over those impeccably choreographed scenes. Having never directed a film, Jonny wanted to rehearse everything far more than one generally does for a movie, which was great for me. The cast was knockout—we had a fairly instant connection with one another and spent the majority of our time in stitches. I felt lucky to work with the likes of Eileen Brennan and Michael McKean. In addition to being thoughtful in terms of my housing, Madeline was one of the funniest people I've ever worked with. She improvised the iconic line about the "flames on the side of my face," which is usually the first thing that gets mentioned about the film now. When she first delivered that line, we all lost it; it was just brilliant. We had to scrape ourselves off the ground. She knew her own mind, Madeline.

Everyone was great fun, really. There are also some quite stylish performances in that film and such strong talent, which inevitably upped the ante. That energy kept everybody on their toes, which brought each scene to its optimum potential. The sense of camaraderie was especially appreciated when I was running amok, knocking people over and making rapid assumptions about who the murderer was...with four different outcomes. No matter what happened, the cast stayed with me and followed my lead.

Wrecked as I was, I had a ball.

Officially, *Clue* had three endings (but we shot four). In each ending, a different culprit was to blame, just as each time you play the game, there's a different murderer, weapon, and locale. In one of the endings, I killed everybody—which was my favorite to shoot. I just got to run around the house maniacally, murdering the lot of them. Sadly, that was the one that got cut, which I understood: it was too obvious and convenient to have the butler do it.

Per Jonny's direction, I narrated each of those endings at a wild pace that really called on all the vigor and stamina I had in my body. In fact, toward the end of the shooting, after running around the house reconstructing the murders, I felt quite ill so they sent me to the nurse. She informed me that my blood pressure was through the roof.

"My God," she said, "you could have had a heart attack!"

Such high-energy performance work takes a toll. In this case, however, it was absolutely worth it.

When it was initially released, you would see a different ending depending on which cinema you attended, and at which time. I thought that was a wonderfully clever and amusing device, but people didn't take to it at the time. Critics are so often averse to innovation. Still, it was very disappointing for it to be so underappreciated. I really felt for Jonny.

Its poor reception eventually worked in its favor—at least in my opinion. I think one of the reasons it was later regarded as a cult classic was because the mainstream didn't initially "get it." Once it was released on VHS, with all of the endings included, subcultures of viewers got the chance to see it on their own terms and form their own rituals around it. It's gone very much in the direction of *The Rocky Horror Picture Show*, in that the movie initially flopped, then has gradually built into something of an underground classic, with genuinely rabid fans who know every line. And, to make a long story short (*too late!*): to see it have such a long life after its debut, appealing to more and more viewers with each passing year, has been incredibly satisfying.

Chapter Fifteen

"When You're Down Here with Me, You'll Float, Too"

(*It*)

I DIDN'T VOLUNTEER OR AUDITION FOR THE ROLE OF PENNY-wise. I didn't audition for a lot in those days; at a certain point, they just send you a script and cross their fingers. And that suited me just fine, as it meant my take on a character could be a surprise.

When my agent asked if I would be interested in the role of a psychotic clown, I was instantly intrigued; it felt like a risk that extended beyond the bounds of my comfort zone. The television adaptation of *It* was based on Stephen King's famous novel, which features a demon that lives in the sewer and terrorizes the townspeople by turning into their worst fears.

The most notable risk factor of this whole undertaking is that I loathe clowns—not quite to the extent that I literally couldn't look at myself in the mirror, as has often been reported, but I certainly didn't delight in my reflection. In any case, the thought of embodying this killer clown made me feel simultaneously uncomfortable *and* like I would be pushing myself to take it on. So, with much uncertainty, the type of which confirmed I was still attempting to embrace my contradictions, I replied: "Yes, I'm interested."

I haven't had much to say about it publicly for many years, which many people misread as my carrying some sort of deep conflict about the role. That's really not the case, but I didn't revel in the role, either. I have great respect for Stephen King and think it's a strong adaptation, but it wasn't exactly a Stoppard experience. Nor did I expect it to be.

Furthermore, it's quite peculiar to discuss being the source of many children's (and adults') nightmares. The majority of people who want to talk to me about being Pennywise are either notably odd people, who sort of revel in his evilness, or else they want me to know that I've really traumatized them, or made it impossible to sleep, or something of that variety. I don't blame them—one of my lines is literally "I'm your worst dream come true." But I've never really known how to respond to that. It's not the most charming conversation starter, and invariably leads to a less than delightful discussion to navigate.

I felt very lucky to have been offered the role, however. There were a number of other very talented people in the running, including Alice Cooper. And indeed, *It* proved to be another super opportunity, and one I hope I made the most of. It was directed by a man named Tommy Lee Wallace, whom I really liked. He knew exactly what he wanted, and offered very specific, lucid direction on how to reach that. Then I could deliver, which is a very satisfying way to work. At the same time, he gave me a lot of room to interpret this very unusual character however I saw fit.

In order to play out Tommy's specific vision, I focused almost entirely on the script, and didn't actually read the novel until afterward. I loved it; it's an odd book, and such a smart idea. I've never met Stephen King himself, but years later, when I was doing some sort of convention, maybe in LA, somebody brought me a first edition of the paperback with a personalized message to me from Stephen. I still treasure it to this day.

As fascinating as I found the character, I can't say I was thrilled to learn that I would have to wear prosthetic makeup, given my *Legend* experience; luckily, Pennywise's makeup was a cakewalk in comparison to becoming Darkness. And when you're wearing makeup that makes you (hopefully) unrecognizable from yourself, there's a different kind of freedom, one that I really enjoy.

Ultimately, *It* is very original, very audacious, and yes, legitimately frightening. My favorite detail was that Pennywise emerges from still photographs from another time, which is a terrifying premise but also so fantastical that it felt like play. I never would have imagined that out of my whole body of work, that clown would end up being so memorable to audiences.

But perhaps that's because I was never really one for the horror genre. My old friend Richard O'Brien was, but I never quite got it. I love subtle psychological horror, more in the realm of

Hitchcock, I suppose. I've never been especially drawn to gratu-
itous effects and absurd gore. I think it's very unfortunate when
flashy makeup and camera tricks take the place of actors who
can actually channel somebody truly psychotic or murderous.

Shows what I know. Audiences took to Pennywise in a way
I *never* could have imagined. At most of the conventions that
I've attended since, there will be at least a couple of fans who
want me to replicate the voice that haunted their dreams as a
child. It's quite a weird phenomenon. I love the idea that, for
example, Frank gave people license to forgo societal limits and
expectations so they could embrace their true selves. I'm still not
sure what Pennywise offered people, other than terror and a reticence about going near sewers. Perhaps you can tell me.

I will say that *It* has an incredibly disappointing ending, in
my opinion. I hope this isn't ruining anything for anybody, but
I feel enough time has passed that I can say it involves a spider
that's really not very scary at all. But an actor's opinion is quite
irrelevant when it comes to such matters.

As for the compassion or connection I felt for Pennywise?
I sympathized with his madness, which is a quality that pre-
sents in many forms. I don't think anybody would find it difficult
to see that in him. I certainly didn't find it challenging to feel
for him. The art of Pennywise is largely tied to him knowing
how to lure and seduce his prey. That is his power and it's what
makes him so terrifying.

That is perhaps why I was less than impressed with the
remake that came out in 2017, which relies far too heavily on
special effects and doesn't leave room for the power that can
be yielded through one's eyes and expression. The capacity
to beckon without words, even as the audience knows they

shouldn't follow—*that* is compelling. I found it a shame to see how many effects were used, precisely because I like and respect Bill Skarsgård very much as an actor, and I felt he would have done a super job had he been given more liberty to embody that power.

Sadly, I never got to know the late Jonathan Brandis (who played the lead role of Bill Denbrough) very well when I was working with him on *It*. It is a strange thing about working with child actors: you either develop a relationship or you don't. This was a particularly unusual situation because there were so many children. I tried to bring as much levity as I could, while also playing the part of... their worst nightmare. But there's only so much you can do.

There's a point at the beginning of the movie where Brandis's fictional younger brother, Georgie (played by Tony Dakota), loses his paper boat, which goes down the drain. Pennywise is there to catch it and to catch him. Georgie puts his hand down and I grab it and suggest that he join me "down here" in the sewer.

During one of the takes, little Tony stopped me in the middle and said, in a very sweet voice, "Mr. Currrrry... you're scaring me."

"I'm sorry, but that's what I'm supposed to be doing. You're *supposed* to be scared," I told him. But I felt bad about it, of course, in a way that I never would have had I been told the same thing by an adult actor.

———

I never set out to be the Prince of Halloween. But there are consequences to agreeing to play the Lord of Darkness, Pennywise, or a Grand Wizard—among many other rather vindictive, unsavory characters.

To play a villain well demands that you dig into dark, weird, fantastical nooks of your own mind, the tabernacles that everyday polite society would rather you not explore. I'm not recommending that you pursue those disconcerting spaces for recreation, but those are pockets where I've uncovered some of my most potent contradictions. They've enabled me to better understand myself, but I wouldn't advocate for everyone to do the same.

I appreciate that villains are often the characters that threaten to sweep you off your feet. Bad guys are sexy. And if I look dashing in the costumes, forgive me; I just can't help it.

But it's not all quite as liberating as you might think. The vocation of playing unusual characters has attracted some extremely unusual attention over the years. The saddest cases are those who exist on the fringe of society, who have perhaps come to feel a true affinity with one of the fictional villains I've played. Those people have often been unwilling to distinguish between who I am and whom I pretend to be, leading to difficult scenarios. I've had a handful of death threats from some rather desperate superfans. I was stalked for a time.

Fortunately, those situations have been outliers. The overwhelming majority of encounters and feedback I've had over the years has been respectful, generous, and surprising... anything but evil.

Chapter Sixteen

"Leaning on a Lamppost"

(*Me and My Girl*)

B ACK IN 1987, A FEW YEARS BEFORE I TOOK ON THE ROLE OF Pennywise, I spent a brief stint in landlocked Eureka Springs, Arkansas, playing a rather unsavory televangelist (who avails himself of most of the Choir of Angels) in a film called *Pass the Ammo*. The experience was largely made possible because my costar and friend Annie Potts played my wife, Darla (who had been modeled on Tammy Faye Bakker, the televangelist). Annie and I had great fun together, staying in a very curious hotel that had clearly been some kind of grimy brothel: it had an inordinate number of bathrooms and a Jacuzzi in every suite.

Mike Ockrent and Gillian Gregory, the director and the choreographer for a forthcoming production of the musical *Me and My Girl*, came to see me while I was on set, which was quite flattering. They told me they'd be touring the States with the show and asked me to star in it as the protagonist, Bill Snibson, a Cockney fellow who learns that he's the fourteenth heir in line to the Earl of Hareford. The proposal struck me as a very convenient response to my unspoken desire: I'd been doing rather alternative films for a while and had been longing to get back to the theater, especially with a show that would be touring major cities, many of which I'd never visited. I also wanted to see what I could do with such a role. So I gratefully agreed.

In more cynical (and entirely accurate) interviews, I've referred to it as my "Get Rich and Get Thin Tour." Not a savory stance but, truth be told, it didn't hurt in either of those departments.

I've had a number of special relationships with brilliant directors over the course of my life, and Mike Ockrent was another one. He'd had a great career back in England and had worked on Stephen Sondheim's smash-hit musical *Follies* and a few other successful gigs on Broadway. Throughout the tour, though we had a very intense schedule and regime, with traveling in between, he gave me a long leash—which I deeply appreciated.

I never would have been able to handle the schedule and the exertion of energy required to keep it up for (in my case) a year if not for the exuberant response from the audience. They gave so much. But as an actor, you can't just rely on a happy crowd to boost you up. You also need to have a strong relationship with your cast and especially with your director.

When the show debuted in New York, Robert Lindsay—a superb actor—originated the role of Bill. I was very conscious of being in his shadow, because I actually went and saw him play the role. Afterward, I met with Mike at a restaurant in New York and noted that it could have been called *Robert Lindsay and Me*. The titular "My Girl" didn't get much of a look in the script. I wanted the musical to be more centered in the relationship, and not just be two and a half hours showcasing my character Bill. I couldn't have done that eight times a week. I wasn't interested in a solo show.

So adjustments were made, not to the script itself but to the direction and choreography. Namely, I had to learn to tap dance—but I enjoyed it because Gillian Gregory was great and very, very patient with me. It's a peculiar thing to learn because tap dancing is all about balance and ankles (and hopefully you have strong ones). Mike had also worked out some very specific pieces of comic business that he wanted me to use, and that was actually quite fun. And there was also this very romantic, almost balletic, scene by a lamppost. I felt like a sort of Fred Astaire, or perhaps Gene Kelly in *Singin' in the Rain*, which I absolutely loved because it reminded me of the American movies and musicals I'd adored as a child. The musical was initially written for a famous comedian back in the thirties. At the time, it was a big ol' hit, though I don't know whether he tap-danced for the role. (I suspect not.)

If you're going to do a musical on the road, *Me and My Girl*'s ideal, because it's full of joy. Musicals can be very daunting, but when they're done well, they incite the kind of pure escapist joy that no other genre can match. The show was a revival, though firmly set in late 1930s England, and playing the happy-go-lucky, tap-dancing Bill was a delightful leap from the more sinister work I'd been doing over the past few years. It was a nice exhale to play the good guy for a change, a bit like playing to my best instincts. He's such a sweetheart, sort of oddly naive and exuberant. That noted, I would eventually get a little bored with dear Bill, because his relentless cheer and extroverted goodness meant we had so little in common.

I also enjoyed sharing the stage with Donna Bullock; even though she was from Waco, Texas, she managed to pull off a believable Cockney accent, which was quite a stretch. She was a really good singer, too. I don't think either of us were great dancers, really, but we pulled it off. And most of all, I did love touring. At least at first. What better way to get to know a country than to travel through it as a sort of joy merchant?

Oddly enough, though I loved being onstage, I suffered practically paralyzing stage fright multiple times across the show's run. I've always adored being on the road, but having to generate that merriment night after night took a real toll on me, and my nerves responded with a sustained bout of legitimate terror. It came out of nowhere. I mean, I was exhausted. But I had been exhausted before. I had experienced the jitters before. This was something else. It came on all of a sudden one night—though I honestly can't remember exactly where I was. I just started shaking in the wings before I was due to go on. I was genuinely worried that I was going to skip onto stage and have an instant heart attack and die. Lest you think I was merely indulging my more dramatic tendencies, you should know that's *truly* how I felt.

Back when I did *Travesties* in London, a friend shared with me that his doctor said that the amount of adrenaline an actor experiences on the first night of a show is enough to give someone a heart attack and die. It's certainly true, but I think that's also one of the reasons you fall in love with theater—the sheer adrenaline of it. It can even feel a bit addicting at times, though of course when it ramps up to stage fright, it's a bit *too* high.

I always managed to get through it, largely thanks to the engagement with the crowd, but I was excessively relieved at the end of every performance. Then the same feeling would come back to immobilize me the next night.

There could have been some logic behind my fright: I was returning to the stage after being in the movies for a while, and I was preoccupied by being in love. But it doesn't altogether make sense that *this*, of all performances, would be the one that would send me into such a tailspin. Whether through heartbreak or breaking hearts—everything translates into my work. Particularly any strength of feeling. I've always tried to be disciplined about not letting anything get in the way of my performance. I can usually leave the outside world behind me.

In hindsight it's amusing, absurd even, given that I was well into my stride and comfortable in the part, which was such a bubble bath compared to any of the classical work that I'd done in the past. But it got quite bad, to the point where I felt completely out of control. When it didn't go away after a few shows, I ended up confiding in Mike and a few others. When we landed in Washington, DC, I went to see a very kind psychiatrist; he gave me half of a Klonopin that I could take *just in case*, and I kept it in my pocket for that very reason. It felt like insurance, and somehow it calmed me just to know it was there. I never actually needed to take it, and I managed to avoid crumbling into a heap mid-song-and-dance as soon as I was out onstage. In time, the fright retreated.

Nerves are an inevitable part of performing. It's not a bad thing to have a sense of occasion and to believe that what you're doing matters enough to scare you. But it's not a fun sensation, and there's a distinction between performance angst and full-blown, incapacitating stage fright. Either way, you can't dwell in it. Especially not when there's an audience of eight hundred people waiting to see you sing and dance and entertain.

Just get out there. You'll remember, "Well, of course, this is what I do." That's at least what I would tell myself, just so I could do it all over again the next day.

It's a more common phenomenon than you might expect among even our most esteemed actors. Laurence Olivier, among other masters, increasingly felt that he couldn't live up to expectations, fearing that audiences would expect a god when he could only ever be a man.

I later read a story about Olivier grappling with his stage fright (which I'm now paraphrasing). He spoke with many people about it, including Sybil Thorndike, a British actress who was married to Sir Lewis Casson, who had been much renowned and still was at the time. On one occasion, Olivier asked her, "Do you ever get frightened before going onstage?"

"Of *course* I do," she evidently said. "Take drugs, deaaar! That's what Lewis and I do."

I imagine she meant some kind of tranquilizer. But it always makes me laugh to imagine this elegant elderly legend scolding Laurence Olivier for not just doing as they did: "*Take drugs*, dear."

It's worth noting that he never did take the drugs, dear—he just got on with it. I never took that half Klonopin, but I did develop other coping mechanisms that proved rather useful. Often, I would just put my head between my knees and breathe really deeply and pretend I was somewhere else. In time, it always passes. Just get on with it. Trust that nerves aren't necessarily negative; they can even be essential.

I had to be onstage for a great majority of the show of *Me and My Girl*, and I didn't just worry about the audience—there was also a cast and a director expecting me to be on cue and on point. My character was sort of meant to carry the performance, or at least to lead from the front. Under different circumstances, I would have cherished that feeling. I love leading a company and being, in significant measure, responsible for the success of a show.

Despite the difficulties, *Me and My Girl* was an immensely valuable experience for me. In addition to learning how to manage my stage fright, it also forced me to get back on the road. It was a long year spent in various cities across America, which offered brilliant education and exposure. And as a lifelong vagabond, I couldn't help but start thinking about where I might end up next.

I loved San Francisco. There was the beauty, of course, but also its lovely, easy pace. There were also plenty of very smart people around, people interested in culture and the arts, which I found quite stimulating. I also adored Sante Fe and New Orleans, but I didn't think moving there more long-term would have been an especially astute career move.

On the other hand, I was decisively *not* a fan of Detroit, likely because it reminded me too much of Birmingham: a Midwestern (and middle-of-the-country, for Birmingham) town, with its main proclivity being motor cars. It didn't help that I stayed in a horrible hotel with very thick glass windows that looked onto the river, which would've been nice—if not for the baseless fear I harbored that one day I was just going to run headfirst into one of those glass windows and never be heard from again. Detroit wasn't a total loss, though; I must admit it has great Greek food. Who knew?

When we at last settled in for an extended run at the Pantages Theatre in Los Angeles, something in me finally clicked. It felt so natural to be there that I finally made a solid decision I'd been leaning toward for some time: to move out to California.

Me and My Girl also proved to be a crucial turning point for me in a very unexpected way, too. While I was on that tour, I was approached by a man called Gordon Hunt—Helen Hunt's father—who was the dialogue director at Hanna-Barbera. They were taking a different route than the standard fare of Flintstones and Yogi Bear by preparing a series of Bible stories. Gordon asked me to be the voice of the serpent in some animated version of the creation of man. I agreed to it with a bit of a shrug, not foreseeing that I would love it as much as I did, or that it would lead to such a vital addition to my bag of tricks.

While I prepared to launch into the world of animation for the first time, I continued to entertain the dream that I would be able to live between Los Angeles and London. But with time, I would learn to accept it was simply too far and too expensive. And so, I put away my tap shoes and prepared to return to normalcy: as an elocution teacher, a concierge, a cardinal, and a Romanian conman.

Chapter Seventeen

"Well, Look at Us, Jim! We're a Festival of Conviviality!"

(*Muppets* and the Mainstream)

I WAS EAGER TO THROW MYSELF INTO THE VOICEWORK AND explore an entirely new genre. But before, and really throughout, doing that, I was being approached to feature in a number of big commercial films that were released in the 1990s. Something about embodying a deranged psychotic clown or an excessively chipper song-and-dance man, and bringing those characters home every night, had left me rather eager to play somebody with a touch more balance—and on solid ground.

Oscar delivered that to me. It's a film that I hold very close to my heart for reasons that aren't even entirely clear to me. It was perhaps among the least successful of my commercial roles in the nineties, in terms of box-office standards. Luckily, I don't run a box office.

Oscar was not commercial if you're looking at numbers. But I'm never looking at numbers (bless you, Cindella, my business manager and beloved friend). The cast was quite well known, which is absolutely not to suggest that it was the most talented group of actors I've ever worked with. Enough cattiness. Suffice to say that I felt a great fondness for the quirky character whom I play in the film.

Oscar is actually a remake of a French film from the late 1960s, but the modern version was set in Chicago. I played Dr. Thornton Poole, a sweet, if horrifically awkward, gentleman who plays the love interest as well as the elocution teacher for Sylvester Stallone's Angelo "Snaps" Provolone. Sly's character hires me to clean up his English and make him sound coherent. I dare say both actor and role could have used such a teacher.

My convenient (and genuine) belief about villains being more interesting to play due to superior writing was turned on its head by my experience in *Oscar*. Though relatively unknown, it holds up among my most enjoyable movies. Part of the fun was definitely that it was directed by my friend John Landis (who'd been initially slated to direct *Clue*). We work together tremendously well, which of course makes a massive difference.

It also helped that I didn't have to stretch into entirely foreign territory for the role, nor did I have to wear prosthetics, nor did I have to tap into wells of malevolence or darkness in order to deliver on my character. Elocution and diction have always been important to me. Language is precious. It

Tim onstage at Headliners in Madison, WI, during his *Fearless* tour, 1979. *Photo courtesy of Jeff Weiland*

Tim and Susan Sarandon after Tim's performance in *Pirates of Penzance* at the Theatre Royal in London, 1978. *Photo courtesy of Getty Images Premium Archive / David Montgomery*

Tim and Ian McKellen in
Amadeus on Broadway, 1980.
Photo courtesy of Zoë Dominic

Tim as the Pirate King in
Pirates of Penzance at the
Royal Theatre in London, 1982.
Photo courtesy of Zoë Dominic

Tim as Bill Snibson in *Me and My Girl* on Broadway, for which he was
nominated for a Tony Award, 1986. *Photo courtesy of Ron Scherl / ArenaPAL*

Tim and Annie Potts in *Pass the Ammo*, 1987. *Photo courtesy of United Archives GmbH / Alamy Stock Photo*

Tim, Seth Green, and Brandon Crane behind the scenes during the filming of *It*, 1990. *Photo courtesy of Brandon Crane with thanks to Gary Smart*

Tim and his niece Kate on the Red Carpet at the 67th Annual Academy Awards, 1995. *Photo courtesy of WWD / Getty Images*

Tim as King Arthur in *Spamalot* on Broadway taking his curtain call on opening night, 2005. *Photo courtesy of UPI / Alamy Stock Photo*

Tim and Eric Idle, with Hannah Waddingham in the background, on the first day of rehearsals for *Spamalot* in London, 2006. *Photo courtesy of Catherine Ashmore*

Tim as Billy Flynn in the television series *Criminal Minds*, 2010. © *2010 American Broadcasting Companies, Inc. All rights reserved (ABC Studios/Randy Holmes)*

Tim and Marcia Hurwitz at a Tony Awards viewing party where Tim received an Artistic Achievement Award from the Actors Fund, 2015. *Photo courtesy of Tim Curry's personal collection*

Tim and Cindy Hudson at Los Angeles City Hall on *Rocky Horror Picture Show* Day commemorating its fortieth anniversary, 2015. *Photo courtesy of Tim Curry's personal collection*

Tim and Charlie Adler filming a Tim Curry Fanmio Experience, 2018. *Photo courtesy of Fanmio*

disturbs me (perhaps more than it should) when people mispronounce words or abbreviate them unnecessarily. That's been entrenched into me. However pretentious or old-fashioned that may seem to others, I loathe when language isn't used properly. I don't know nor do I care to pinpoint why that got lodged into me: Is it because I'm English? Was it something I was taught? Is it because my vocation has always relied on its proper use? Frankly, it does not matter. When you're acting, you have the privilege of making somebody's words come alive. That's a responsibility and an honor that I embrace with such fervor that I have now, in this very paragraph, become incredibly verbose trying to explain why I do not need to explain myself.

For a movie set as low-key and "normal" as *Oscar*, it started in quite a dramatic fashion: the very first night that I was shooting there, much of the studio, including my dressing room, burnt down—literally to the ground.

My mother phoned me soon after, having seen reports of it on the news. If you believe she was calling because of a deep-rooted concern for my livelihood . . . then you haven't been reading very closely.

"When did it happen?" she asked warily.

"After we'd gone home for the evening," I replied.

There was a long pause, then she responded, in a rather accusatory tone that was so familiar to me, "You weren't *smoking*, were you, darling?"

As to my connection with Mr. Thornton Poole, elocution tutor extraordinaire, I held a deep understanding of and empathy for his shyness and lack of social grace. I also felt great compassion for his difficulties with talking to a woman. I still consider the role as a real gift, because Thornton, as a human being, had a clean slate. Remember: this was 1991, and I had many things in my life, but a clean slate was not among them. Especially when your livelihood falls into the lane of having some kind of celebrity status, and even more so if you have a conscience, whatever roles you inhabit linger; they stay with you, to some degree. If you care enough to want to persuade people (or persuade yourself) that you're *not* a given character, you have to play the next one with just as much authenticity. You have to play it purely. Regardless, I loved leaning into the notion of innocence when I was playing Thornton.

It was also a relief not to be too Technicolor about it all. I embraced how low-key the production was (once the fumes had cleared, anyway), especially compared with so much of my more over-the-top work. That pace was just what I needed at that point in time. I never thought it was going to have a big future, and I was correct about that. But I liked my character a lot, even though I struggled a bit with my fellow cast members.

There were some very odd choices in casting, from my vantage. Sylvester Stallone was having a go at a comedic role. I *think*. He was not especially articulate, and didn't need to be—perhaps he was method acting, or perhaps he was simply OK with being Sylvester Stallone. Who can say? I do remember that he was always fucking girls in his dressing room, which should've been none of my business—though the noises and general traffic ended up making it *everybody's* business. Marisa Tomei, my supposed love interest, was not a kindred spirit, either—to my disappointment. So it wasn't a jolly camaraderie among the cast that inspired my affection.

In the end, it made sense that it was not a real blockbuster success, however much I enjoyed playing a mild-mannered fellow. Maybe I was kidding myself by playing somebody so virtuous.

———

Though my next major film was still light and commercial, I returned to playing a foil when cast in *Home Alone 2: Lost in New York*, which was shot almost immediately following *Oscar* and came out in 1992. The sequel to the popular Christmas movie was essentially a recreation of the first, except instead of holding down the fort in his own home, Kevin (of course played by Macaulay Culkin) is left to fend for himself while alone in New York's Plaza Hotel. I play the stiff, stuffy, extremely British concierge, Mr. Hector. As the Plaza's concierge, I'm deeply suspicious of Kevin and refuse to keep my nose out of his business. Younger generations seem to truly revere the movie, which I trust must be in large part due to the nostalgia felt for the original *Home Alone*.

Home Alone 2 was a lovely treat, partly because it was delightful to be in New York during Christmas. And we were all lucky enough to stay at the Plaza. I'm not sure if the rooms were allotted based on hierarchy, but mine had a view of a brick wall. I didn't make too much out of that. It was a luxurious perk and indicative of the budget for the film, which was certainly not lacking.

Early in the shooting, Ivana Trump came around and asked me what I thought of the decor of the hotel, which she had played a central role in redesigning. Unfortunately, I was forced to lie. Because the truth is that there is a beautiful

black-and-white terrazzo floor in the lobby, but she had made
the baffling decision to cover it up with a very florid carpet that
was positively ghastly. Or maybe that was her vision of a fancy
hotel. Later in the week, Donald Trump and Marla Maples—
who was his mistress at the time—did a walk-through while we
were shooting one of the scenes, eager to find the director.

"I want Marla to meet Chris Columbus," Trump said to me,
"because Marla is a *very* talented actress."

"I'm...sure she is," I said, leaning fully into the conciliatory
tone of a typical top-notch concierge. That wasn't a complete lie;
I have no doubt she was good at faking it.

I liked Chris Columbus as a director. He gave me free rein to
play the character however I wanted. At this point in my career,
I appreciated that kind of room. And my role, at least compar-
atively speaking, was very straightforward, quite silly, entirely
harmless. A good director can sort of smell it when the actors
need more assistance or less. I've had plenty of mediocre screen
directors over the years who would ask too much from actors:
"Now...take three steps to the left...and now one to the right."
That just wasn't necessary in this case, and Chris and I were
both aware of it, which made the whole experience much better
for both of us, I believe.

Acting along with Macaulay Culkin was interesting from
a procedural perspective, though tiresome, because he tended
to gabble. By that I mean he'd spew out his lines without very
much thought. As mentioned, I'm devoted to actors using the
words on the page, so that drove me a little crazy, but it wasn't
my place to critique him. Any annoyance I may have felt about
him wasting others' time didn't hurt our characters' dynamic,
either, and I understood that he was coming from a different

place of celebrity and of course a very different age. (He was only eleven or twelve at the time.)

Macaulay also had his own room at the Plaza, as we were filming there. He would watch TV all night, I imagine just as Kevin might have, so he was rarely in the best shape the next morning. He would sort of stumble into the makeup trailer as though he'd been on a three-day bender. It was obvious that he was just exhausted.

Columbus was very tolerant of that behavior and used to stand beside the camera and play the other parts to coach Macaulay's performance. In my opinion, he could have used a bit more of the "three steps to the left" style of direction. But Chris was very forgiving. Or just assumed that he would handle it in the editing. Personally, I liked Macaulay, and I have a lot of sympathy for child actors, so I did strive to be patient with him. I hope I succeeded. Many child actors—understandably—don't know what the hell they're doing there, really. By the early 1990s, young Macaulay had achieved widespread celebrity status and was recognized everywhere. I find that strange as an adult, so I can't imagine what it must have been like to process it as a kid.

Joe Pesci was back as one of the two villains who are after Kevin. Pesci and I did not especially get on. Oil and water, really, in terms of our personalities. We never had any specific issues or anything, nor did we spend much time engaging with each other when we didn't need to. He's a tough guy, and the rage he exhibits so brilliantly onscreen seems to come very naturally to him. So much so that it made me think of the childhood experiences I've tapped into myself—and made me wonder if there's something he carries with him at all times, too.

For the most part, however, *Home Alone 2* was just a jolly, light production. I quite enjoyed myself, and it seemed to make a lot of people happy. It still does. It was a very different kind of acting experience for me, one that I wouldn't have thought I would enjoy as much as I did. But I remain proud of it, and I'm delighted that it brought people simple joy and distraction.

The stage always lures me back if I spend too much time away, but after a brief spell on Broadway in the musical *My Favorite Year*, I went abroad to star in another flashy, commercial movie for Walt Disney's *The Three Musketeers*. Every generation seems to feel compelled to have a go at the classic, and I loved the book as a boy, so I was eager to bring it to life, especially for younger viewers. I didn't step in as one of the swashbucklers, but instead was cast as the rather grandiose, detestable, strangely seductive Cardinal Richelieu. We shot in Vienna, and I had a lot of fun sweeping around the gorgeous capital in long red robes, flinging my cloak around and channeling a sort of Dracula-esque character.

We first went to Rome for costume fittings, which I was of course thrilled to do; any journey to Italy is a journey worth taking. Being abroad also gave me a chance to get the measure of my costars, including Charlie Sheen. Not the sharpest pencil in the drawer, Charlie. Loved his drink, though I did as well and can't throw any stones in that department. Perhaps it was for the best that we never meshed well enough to partake of our booze together. He recruited one of the other cast members to be his drinking buddy, which would have been fine, but the first assistant director used to have to drag them out of less virtuous establishments in the morning so that we could get to work.

The tricky thing with some of these villainous characters, even of the Disney variety, is that they have a capacity to hang around and become a part of you. If you're not careful about the boundary between work and reality, you can reach a stage when you are forced to kick them out. You cannot continue letting them come home with you. Though I did not realize in real time how thoroughly engaged with him I was becoming, in retrospect, I can see that I reached that point with Cardinal Richelieu. I had a wonderful time playing him, especially because we did so in Vienna and I was delighted to be in a new city. But as much as I enjoyed being in Europe and flinging Richelieu's cape around, I often felt him creeping into my personal life, which I didn't want at all.

Cardinal Richelieu definitely ranks among my most villainous characters, though he often gets overlooked in that category. I had to be careful about not trying to be too clever while playing him. I had fun with it, but he is by no means a kind character—particularly with women. I was not wild about taking that on all that much. He is very seductive and very sure of himself, and though it can be quite fun to play somebody like that from time to time, I dare say I've had my fill of embodying such characters.

———

Shortly after wrapping up *The Three Musketeers* in 1993, I was cast as Herkermer Homolka in *Congo*, which was directed by Frank Marshall, who'd already produced a lot of Spielberg's work. For a producer, he made a fine director, and did so in tandem with his wife, Kathleen Kennedy. Neither the film nor my role begs to be written about, though—in fact, it's perhaps the worst picture I ever made. Or, at least, I do not consider it a script that anyone would rush to bind in leather.

I've actually seen it on a plane, which is where I would advise people to seek it out, if they're planning to watch it all. People have spoken to me about it in positively glowing terms, which tells me a lot about that person. Perhaps it's worth revisiting, but there are so many better films to watch. I am being overly harsh. Of course it had some merits.

I have absolutely no regrets about having done it—I don't waste time regretting *any* of the performances that I was in, especially when they involved a strong cast, which *Congo* did. Laura Linney is a great actress, and I liked her well enough. But we didn't spend our time on set laughing uproariously. She is extremely serious about her work, and has that very distinct voice that for some reason resounds in my mind as being a Connecticut accent (even though she is from New York). She has an interesting history of acting on both stage and screen and, had I felt the film was worthy of it, I would have had nothing but respect for how earnestly she took on the role.

My memory struggles with pinpointing the specific characteristics of the film that made it a notably redeeming experience, but its endurance with audiences (according to my accountant and based on how often I've been asked about it) makes me inclined to try to understand why.

I suppose I enjoyed that it was something different, and different is always valuable. Costa Rica was also very nice, though I was disappointed that we never went to Africa for a movie named *Congo*. (I trust for financial reasons.)

In the end, I probably have myself to blame for many of the struggles I encountered on the set. I knew I would be climbing volcanos while filming it yet was still resolutely smoking two packs of Marlboros a day. Which, you may be surprised to learn, doesn't vibe terrifically well with climbing volcanos. The scenery was spectacular, and we got to shoot a lot of it from great heights, which was nice.

As you have gathered, I did not weep when we wrapped.

———

Having had the privilege to play many different types of characters, I struggle with the rather impossible question of my favorite role. I've never been able to offer a consistent, satisfying answer whenever people ask for the superlatives: my best, my worst, the closest to my nature, the furthest from it. My response changes based on the time of the year or time of day. That I have so many to choose from is an incredible privilege. I know how lucky I have been.

However, I *can* always say, unequivocally, that one of the best pictures I ever made—or at least a top contender for the most delightful cinematic experience I've enjoyed, and most certainly the apex of my big films from the 1990s—came along when director Brian Henson (the son of the legendary Jim Henson) was searching for somebody to play Long John Silver in his new Muppet movie, *Muppet Treasure Island*.

They needed somebody who could play an extravagant, boisterous, duplicitous character who could also sing. It helped immensely that I already loved the Muppet franchise; it's just a world of fun and I'd been glued to the TV show. I had no hesitation about working with them.

I cannot overstate how much I adored working with the Muppets. The extraordinary thing about them is that they are all characters in their own right, and you should treat them as such. It also helped that I was in the upswing of my voice acting endeavor—my respect for my fellow actors was immense.

More than anything, though, I had *such* a good time. The Muppet universe is truly one of a kind, and it is damn impressive what they can do. If you have the privilege, and you allow yourself to enter their world, it really does not take long to forget that you are working with puppets. They are *actors*, each filled with distinct characteristics and foibles and all of our very human traits. (As am I—I was informed while writing this book that there is a popular meme in which the internet speculates I was successful in the film because I considered myself a "fellow Muppet." Absolutely not.)

My favorite was always Gonzo, who was always the victim, and never deserved it. I pity him. I also have a fondness for Miss Piggy, who's quite a seductive girl. She's always funny, and *never* boring. Although I did say at the outset that I wouldn't speak about any of my romantic relationships, I will say that Miss Piggy and I had *quite* a good time together, both on set and in our trailers. Fortunately, our dalliances never led to any tension with Kermit—I was clever about it.

One of the main reasons these characters are so memorable is because the Muppeteers, who literally breathe life into them and control their voices and movements, are utterly brilliant. They improvise a lot and are given the liberty to do so, which added to the fun of being given the opportunity to join them. They're an incredibly talented lot and have a ball playing off one another. It's a contagious atmosphere of delight and artistry.

Though working among puppets (again, if you're adaptable) becomes normal quickly enough, it does take a bit of getting used to—at least in the beginning. One of the major adjustments of the production was being on a boat for much of the filming, which meant that the Muppeteers were mostly squatting on the floor, because they had hollowed out parts of the boat so that they could stand up and do all the mechanisms and work out the physical relationships while doing the voices at the same time. Imagine the skill it requires to be so funny and identifiable while all of that is being asked of you.

As for me, I didn't really have a process to speak of for inhabiting the character of Long John Silver and playing alongside these creatures. Doing so does require that you have a scope of imagination, I suppose. But I never had any issues with viewing the Muppets as equals. I did have to learn how to be careful and conscientious about *not* seeing the Muppeteers, and to focus my gaze and my attention in such a way that I could only appear to be engaging with the actual Muppets themselves. It helped enormously that the writers were phenomenal, the dialogue engrossing, and the director willing to let us play until we got it right. It was a magical time, if a bit fucking surreal. Plus, Henson and the whole Muppet franchise made for such a generous audience that, for the first time, I sang live on set, without any hesitation or concern about judgment.

As for Long John Silver, he's archetypal, a classic. He's one of the first jolly villains many of us learn about as a child. He's charming, wonderfully self-centered, and not *super* villainous— so there was quite a lot to which I could connect. And even though he seeks to gain young Jim Hawkins's sympathy for nefarious reasons, it helps that there is still a kindness to him,

behind his impishness and greed. It was a little physically tax-
ing, though, as they tied my leg up and I had to learn how to
handily hop around convincingly. Thankfully, I had a crutch,
and not too many active scenes.

When Silver's being kind, it was easier to play the part,
because it was more in keeping with my own nature. Then,
when Silver is revealed as actually being naughty and greedy,
that was more fun and required more intentional acting. So I
got a taste of both. I do love getting a turn at playing the bad
boy, especially in such a harmless production.

I have never been much of an improvisational person. That's
more of an American phenomenon. This film was the one very
memorable exception for me, which was perhaps inspired by the
way the Muppeteers work. There's a script, of course, but they
deviate from it regularly enough that I felt liberated to do the
same. There's a whole improvised scene where Silver is trying to
establish a rapport and relationship between himself and young
Jim. Having lost my father at a similar age, and for that to have
been such a formative time for me, made my heart go out to
Jim's character in a very authentic way. I tried to imagine how
I wished people had spoken to me when I was a boy. There was
nobody in my life who filled that role for me back then. I suppose one or two caring people tried. But I never truly allowed
anyone in. My grieving process was carried out in a very solitary
and confused manner.

So there was a real honesty in how I delivered my lines,
though of course, Silver's motives are less than virtuous; he's
trying to gain the boy's sympathy, or to make himself more lik-
able and accessible so that he can glean whether or not Jim pos-
sesses the coveted treasure map. But ultimately, the kid feels

alone, and I understood just how that felt. I drew from the heart and they let me roll with it.

Opening myself up in such a personal way wasn't something I'd ever really experimented with before in film, and certainly not on the stage. I had not planned on that bit; it just happened. In the end, I was very happy with it, though; it felt like a real risk in a very different kind of way, and I was proud of how I'd pulled it off. It was especially possible because I was genuinely fond of not just Jim, but also Kevin Bishop, the actor who played him. He was sixteen at the time, though he struck me as a bit younger. But he was a real sweetheart and responded so naturally while the cameras kept rolling.

Brian Henson was also a very special director. He really got it and let all of us do our thing. I hope that doesn't sound like I'm giving him less credit than he's due, or like it's some great surprise that he was a terrific director. I have enormous respect for the trust he put in me and the whole cast—Muppets or otherwise. It takes a generous director to allow you to express yourself off the cuff, and then find a way to weave it all together. I don't doubt that it also must have been quite hard to exist in his father's shadow. But I never got the sense that he overcompensated, nor did I think about him in those terms during the time when I was lucky enough to work with him.

After filming wrapped on the project, I missed it very much.

I was genuinely saddened to return to dealing with humans again.

It's funny to hear people talk about iconic films, iconic characters. What does iconic really mean? A very fucking boring and unimaginative way to answer the question is to look at my residuals, but they do offer a decided answer, I suppose. Every quarter, the films that continue to make money are from around this era in the nineties (which is by no means to suggest that they were my favorite): *The Hunt for Red October. Clue. Congo. The Wild Thornberrys.* Sometimes very random appearances like *Charlie's Angels* reappear. (*Rocky Horror Picture Show* is a whole different thing because it is based in the UK.) It's an interesting way to take note of what endures; what the numbers say. They certainly surprise me, as they tend to offer a different read than my own lived experience.

And, of course, looking at these numbers doesn't account for the plays I squeezed in, too, which tended to be where my heart would be wholly engaged. There's just a magic about the theater that can't be replicated through celluloid.

By the end of that rapid-fire succession of films, which had carried me back to New York, to Vienna, and then to Costa Rica, I just wanted to feel settled at home.

Somewhere.

Finally, I settled on LA, which baffled some of my British friends. They just couldn't get their minds around the idea that I'd want to stay there long term.

"Why do you want to go to *LA*?" they'd ask.

"Well," I'd reply, "that's where they point cameras at you."

Chapter Eighteen

Loss in Los Angeles

B Y THE TIME I STARTED SETTLING DOWN IN LA, I FELT confident about being established in the acting world. It seemed fitting, or interesting (at least to me), that my first foray there in my twenties had been when I had broken away from the pack and done something quite radically different with *Rocky Horror*—and that I had returned due to something as mainstream and traditional as *Me and My Girl*.

When I first arrived in California with *Rocky Horror* back in the mid-1970s and was living in Sunset Tower, I found it all quite bewildering. When I moved back to give it another go—after working for a while in the theater in England, then in alternative film, then with the *Me and My Girl* run at the Pantages—California at last stuck with me.

It felt familiar, it felt right, it felt like it was time. I'd been returning for all kinds of work there for about fifteen years, so when I finally determined it was time to tame my vagabond leanings and decide on a place to call home, it did not feel like a big adjustment. I knew what I was in for. Moreover, I would not have made the move had I not had a trusted network of about five really good friends who I knew would always tell me the truth—you need that in Los Angeles, more than anywhere else I've lived.

In reality, there was more to it than just moving "where they point cameras at you." I was also motivated by the sun, and by swimming, and by being back by the ocean, and by having a lovely garden I could tend to year-round. Unlike England, it is very rarely gray in sunny LA, and when it is, it's usually a welcome relief. And again, there were my good, trustworthy friends, many of whom I'd met in the entertainment industry. I liked how easy it was. And I loved that I was constantly working.

I still adore being able to spend so much time outdoors here. Aside from being so close to the industry I love, it's one of the main reasons I've stayed in LA, as inhibited and restricted as my movements now are. I used to savor driving up the freeway, getting off at the Universal City exit, and going in to make a Hollywood movie in a place so completely rich with that legacy.

By the time I had my first home and was fully committed to that change, I found myself uncommonly thrilled about where I was living. The ocean was never far, and I had a pool, a garden, and a dog. Those have been constants for all of my homes in California, without exception.

I'd never had a dog as a child, but I always wanted one very much. I was annoying enough about the request that I was eventually given a toy dog, which I recall as being a grim disappointment. It was utterly shit at playing fetch.

———

My mother and I had sort of learned to get on once we were living on opposite sides of the world. Whenever I visited England, usually to see my sis and my nieces or for a job, I would make sure to go and visit my mother. We developed something of a tradition staying in Plymouth's grandest hotel on the Plymouth Hoe (which is the place where Sir Francis Drake was famously playing bowls in the late sixteenth century when the Spanish Armada arrived). The first time that I took my mum there, there was a tall ship with full sails in the bay that had dropped its anchor. I gather it was some variety of tall-ship convention or some special weekend, because a series of similar vessels showed up. The whole scene made the view appear rather glamorous, which my mother loved. She was probably in her sixties when that tradition started, but we kept it up for years. On a few occasions, which I think began with a touchstone birthday, I called her old friends and invited them to dinner at the hotel. The food was shit and bland as could be, but they all delighted in being there. She was a bit happier with me by then, too—as long as I was footing the bill and showing her and her friends a grand old time.

My mother had always said that she wanted to live to be eighty. And she was nothing if not determined. So of course she *did* make it to eighty—and that was her exact age when she died, due to melanoma. I tried to help take care of her whenever I could, but she did not want me to be her nurse, nor was I particularly eager to fill that role.

She rang me one day, however, and simply said, "I don't want to be here anymore." I didn't know precisely what she meant, but I got on a plane and showed up every day that I could. At that stage, she was primarily being looked after by the Macmillan nurses. They are an organization of palliative care nurses who keep you out of pain, really, and they were just wonderful with her.

She passed away peacefully enough, with the assistance of those gentle souls, in the summer of 1999. Judy and I took her ashes out to sea. Even then, we didn't speak about her all that much; we understood each other's positions when it came to our mother.

Whenever Judy and I were together, whether we were spreading Mum's ashes or driving through towns in Norfolk or whatever, our time was so special that the last thing either of us wanted to do was bring our family into it—either physically or through conversation. I'm sure it could have been very cathartic for us to have a real conversation about our mother, and I would have loved to have learned more about my father through her. I never properly asked her what it was like for her to be the apple of his eye and then to lose him, and I wish I had. But at the time, neither of us needed or really wanted to revisit all of that hurt, and there were more interesting things to discuss.

The much greater shock than my mother passing—and perhaps the greatest tragedy in my life—knocked me over just two years later, when Judy died of a brain tumor at only sixty years old. There is no way to articulate how it felt to lose my sister, who was in many ways my only lifeline back to myself and my roots. I was shattered.

She'd always had awful migraines, just as my father had. The tumor showed up when she was in her fifties, and she fought with the fucker for a few very tough years. I was untethered by the loss, and my brother-in-law and her children were devastated, as to be expected. I still speak to my sis sometimes, though she died more than twenty years ago. It was very lucky that we ended up loving each other as much as we did, because for a while there—primarily when I was her rather eccentric kid brother, four years her junior—she thought I was a real buzzkill. And, as usual, she was not entirely wrong with that assessment.

I long to laugh with her. I don't know whether time heals all wounds; it certainly hasn't healed this one.

However much I resist looking back, I miss Judy all the time.

———

I returned to Los Angeles feeling like less of a person. I was very alone, despite having created a network of wonderful, supportive friends. Though it was cold comfort, I was very grateful to return to the house that I had made into my own.

Many might define a vagabond as somebody who has no home. I'm more inclined to interpret it that any vagabond worth a damn creates many homes in any number of places. Which is what I've done in LA.

Given my deep appreciation for aesthetics, lack of affection for the unreliable houses of my youth, and pockets of time when I had ample resources, I've been compelled to buy and restore a lot of houses over the years. I don't care what you call it: a hobby, a passion, a curiosity. If I'm a passenger in the car, I'm always looking at For Sale signs, no matter where I am. And it has been my great fortune to have owned several homes, moving from one to the next. I genuinely enjoy house hunting. Even if I don't have the desire to buy, I do quite like visiting and just imagining what I could make of it, or what kind of a life I could live there. I'm particularly drawn to those with plenty of room for entertaining and a nice large garden to re-envision—that's a requisite part of the deal.

Gardening has always been my way of getting sane and coming back to myself. It became a passion early in life. When I was younger, creating a garden wherever we went served as a means of carving out my own territory, even if I knew it would be a fleeting space. One house that we moved to when I was probably around seven or eight was a naval quarter, in a new suburb, on a whole development. In short order, my dad went to work making a garden for it. He wasn't really a gardener; he just felt it was his responsibility to do something with the plot because it was brand new. He did lovely borders in the front garden that featured some quite (seemingly) patriotic red, white, and blue flowers.

My mother, on the other hand, could not have cared less. She killed plants regularly. Judy wasn't particularly into it, either. Nevertheless, when I went to see my sis in Norfolk in the first house that they'd bought there, I had to make fun of her for absolutely butchering the bushes. I mean, what she thought of as pruning could only be classified as a kind of ritual slaughter. But I think she meant well. Of course she did not appreciate my critique.

People (particularly in LA) are quick to suggest that gardening's a quintessential English pastime. It's certainly revered there, and generously practiced. For me, though, it's just another form of creativity, one that conveniently doesn't require other people. It's the closest I'll ever get to painting, which I would have loved to have been able to do. (Unfortunately, I have no talent for it whatsoever.) And it's hard to deny it: I've been a very happy, healing man whenever I could spend blissful days in the sun and soil, especially in my California gardens.

I spent a decent amount of time restoring a rather neglected but—in its heart—grand 1920s Spanish house in the Los Feliz area of LA, which is quite near the infamous Hollywood sign. I bought it when it was in desperate need of love and attention, uncovered the original plans for it, and restored it to its original structure, while adding personal touches (sprinkles of mischief) along the way.

I was particularly pleased with the garden, though I can't say that my hands were too deep in the soil (which is a cute way of stating that I had a lot of assistance in getting it up to snuff). But I planted with the intention of leaving behind something beautiful for all those who would follow. I redesigned the outdoor space with two patios; if you were seated at one of them, you could watch the sun rise, while the other was optimum for watching it set. I needed the distraction, and I came to adore it so much, I really did. Unfortunately I would not be able to live in such a home like that in my current state. But it was a gift while I had it, and I sincerely hope its current owners and all those who follow find as much tranquility in that garden as I did.

———

People have often contacted me for roles when they're trying to figure out "Who the hell can play this?" or, more likely, "Who would want to?" I'm brought the roles, then I determine whether I can find a point of connection or compassion.

But I've never had some decision matrix. I haven't spent time evaluating whether I'm making a wise or strategic choice. I trust my gut. It's not always right, but intuition dictates whether I understand some morsel of a given character, then I am driven by curiosity about how I might reflect that. Even when I haven't felt an immediate affinity, the sense of risk impels me. It's always interesting to just charge ahead and show up.

In any scenario, I thrive best with directors who gamble— in an informed, confident manner—with their productions and actors. I've been very lucky to have been sought out or accepted by people like Jim Sharman. Stephen Frears. Peter Wood, who always had the guts to take people from one kind of theater and see what they could do. Ridley Scott, who took a chance and put up with a lot of my shit. (I agreed to wear hooves, so I'd call us even.) John Huston. Jonathan Lynn. John Landis. Mike Nichols. Others whom I'm forgetting. I'm humbled to have worked with all of them.

The hardest thing about acting is finding out who you are in the first place—then filtering your character through your nature and experiences. Audiences can smell when you're not authentic. The stench is overwhelming, and threatens to ruin an entire production.

By my sixties, I didn't have to do many auditions—though that's not to say I disliked doing them, as they can serve as terrific means of self-reflection. If the casting directors don't like what they see, *fuck 'em*. I've been turned away from auditions for being too terrifying. I never know how much of that is people making associations with other characters I've played, or if I just naturally have a more frightening demeanor than intended. I find either potential rather amusing, and quite a good indication that said role was never meant to be.

Regardless of whether you land a part, one of the greatest assets is having a strong advocate in your corner. One you can trust. A hugely significant reason that I have been able to keep up with such a varied mix of acting and voicework entered my life the day I met Marcia Hurwitz, who was initially my commercial agent and now serves as my manager, beloved friend, and de facto family member. She is also a primary reason why I'm still alive and kicking.

Marcia became a part of my life at a crucial juncture. Originally from Brooklyn, now an established manager in LA, she is very protective and very smart. She knows what's up and has always upheld a solid understanding of my druthers, no matter how odd they may be. It has been essential to my livelihood that we also happen to get along brilliantly.

Marcia did it all in the entertainment realm, but when we first met, she specialized specifically in voicework. She did not originally help with my theatrical gigs. She would eventually focus on my films as well—but that was much later. Initially, she handled my voice gigs, which proved crucial when the TV shows and the movie roles were drying up a bit, as they do. Voicework was a welcome constant, and through that new world, Marcia became a regular source of support in my life.

Marcia's late husband, Richard, was a damn good jazz trumpeter and a composer. The three of us got on fabulously and they became like family. We ended up traveling together, especially to Italy, and together relished the good life whenever we were abroad.

After he passed away, she went rogue from her company, and I was happy to go rogue with her. She believes in me fiercely, which I love and appreciate. So when she quit, she became my manager instead of my agent. I was thrilled about that, because I knew she'd fight for me. And she does—even to this day. She always aims high.

Once she became my manager, she found all sorts of opportunities for me that I never would have considered, let alone sought out, otherwise. She never saw a project that wasn't worth doing. I say that with enormous gratitude, as her instincts—plus the assistance of the angelic Cindy Hudson (the aforementioned Cindella)—have ensured that I remain solvent over the years.

Later down the line, Marcia even suggested that I use my voice for video games. It may come as a disappointment to some readers—and to those who care, I apologize for my candor—to learn that I have never been personally interested in video games. I confess—it's a bit more extreme than that, really. I remain utterly mystified by them. I do not have a frame of reference that enables me to understand how to experience it, or what the appeal is. When she first brought up the idea, for a project called *Red Alert 3*, Marcia presented it well, and it sounded like a different, unique leap of sorts. I figured, why the fuck not? Even so, I find it very odd to imagine a bunch of kids playing video games somehow narrated—during exclamatory moments—by my voice.

But apparently, now that video games were becoming practically three-dimensional engagements, there was significant money to be made for celebrities who offered up their talents. And sometimes, as it was with *Red Alert 3*, the parts required more than just voicework. I was up there against a green screen, motion-capped and providing the visuals, too.

Though I'll always prefer stage and camera work, I enjoyed acting against that green screen, which I found to be great fun.

My favorite part of all? *The check.* That was the year of Dom Pérignon and caviar, in an era defined by a very fortuitous combination of commercial films and a steady love affair with the world of voicework.

Chapter Nineteen

"That Was Smashing, Poppet!"

(Voicework)

VOICEWORK IS FASCINATING. I HAD ALWAYS EXPERIMENTED with voices, of course, and adjusted my accent accordingly for all the roles I had played in the past. In a sense, I had been introduced to the concept of it as a child: My primary source of "entertainment" growing up had been the radio, so I have always had great respect for audio. It's a different relationship between you and the audience. A bit like reading, it places much more responsibility on the text and more liberty on the audience to envision characters and scenes. But it's still up to you as an actor to figure out how to best engage an audience's imagination using only your voice, and it can be quite an engrossing exercise.

As a matter of fact, I recommend that you try it. If you're reading this in print or on an e-reader, what are you hearing in your mind's speaker as you peruse these pages? If it's your own voice, try out a few others—perhaps even some of mine.

You have my permission. Nay, my *encouragement.*

Dr. Frank-N-Furter's voice would be a provocative baritone: silky, bold, yet with the underlying intonation of an elderly woman of Knightsbridge who is attempting to sound like the Queen. The deep roar of the Lord of Darkness, however, would be far more demanding and menacing, the likes of which would place a rather incongruous rumble on the earlier chapters about my schoolboy days spent collecting butterflies. The unhinged Pennywise's tone should float into something nasal and abrupt; it's frightening simply because it knows no other way to be. Rooster Hannigan is a gritty American snarl. Butler Wadsworth would probably be the closest to my natural accent, but delivered with more delicacy and elegance, even at its swiftest clip. Long John Silver borrowed my grandfather's accent from southwestern England, while allowing for the slurs of a seafarer. The smashing Nigel Thornberry lands his lines with an upper-class tone—but not an exceedingly stuffy one.

Try them all.

In every role, I've played around with sound in new ways—high and low, fast and slow, elite and pedestrian—all in search of the perfect tone for any particular character.

My first voice role was as the serpent in 1988's *The Greatest Adventure: Stories from the Bible.* I spent a while trying out different voices for the serpent, intrigued by the reality that I would not be able to rely on facial expressions whatsoever to convey the character's true nature to the audience. Of course, the writing relied heavily on the letter *s* and the voice was a hiss, the way that cobras hiss. It also needed to be a seductive sort of voice, and I relied a lot on the director for guidance there.

As for connection, finding compassion wasn't hard at all. I connect quite directly with original sin. I think we all do... some more than others. But he's *malevolent*, that serpent. Nevertheless, I felt well acquainted with original sin and the seduction of evil, personally and professionally.

After having such a fantastic time giving voice to the snake, I thanked Gordon Hunt, who had first approached me with the job offer while I was still performing *Me and My Girl*.

"I've decided to come back to live here in Los Angeles, and would love to do more of that," I told him. I admired Gordon. He was a real gentleman, both kind and extremely clever. Every time Hanna-Barbera was casting a series, he would bring me in, show me a few sketches, and just let me do whatever I wanted with it. It was such fun, and was also quite handy, because I had decided to concentrate exclusively on movies (as opposed to stage work) for a while.

The challenge with films is that even if you do two per year, you're left with months without doing anything, trying to find the next gig or waiting for one to start, inevitably wondering if there *will* be another one. Voicework filled in those gaps, giving me something to do during those lulls and assisting in terms of helping to pay for my rather demanding gardens during pauses in film or television work.

In addition to having a sound knowledge of his field, Gordon was a great appreciator of talent, which I liked because it was always intriguing to observe the way he connected other people's vocal talents to specific characters or stock roles, and then how the animators would play off of that. I never spent too much time dwelling on the fact that while I was up there tap-dancing as Bill Snibson, in one of the most joyous roles of my career, he observed and somehow concluded that I'd be the ideal voice for the instigator of all human sin.

Due to his vision and my own curiosity, I got a foothold in the world of professional voicework. I suppose it was an artistic or creative risk of sorts. I've always enjoyed the pursuit of less-expected paths, and going the way of cartoons had never been on my list of goals. Though it's now practically expected out of mainstream actors, especially comedic ones, it wasn't a common thing to do back then. Animation, of course, has gone through a meteoric rise since then, and has gotten significantly more technical and digitized. It has also become very commonplace for major film actors to cross over.

That just wasn't the case in the late eighties. There were plenty of voice artists who made their steady living out of it, and they were (initially) less than pleased by my encroaching on their territory. Some even raised the issue with me directly and were quite sniffy about me staying in my lane, which I found a little silly. I basically told them to bugger off, very confident in my right to do both, as long as I did them well.

But in fairness, I was accepted into their universe quite quickly, once they realized I was decent at the work and that I took it as seriously as any other kind of acting. As long as we were in the world of humans (I never did plants or animals as well), I loved inventing animated characters' personalities through subtle changes in my voice, and came to greatly respect all of the work that goes into every frame of those productions. And there are SO many frames. It's quite miraculous, the level of dedication that goes into making a decent piece of animated work.

Once I became something of a regular at a couple of the animation studios, including one that was bang in the middle of Hollywood, I adored the time of day after I'd recorded my bit, when I could just meander through the artists' section. There was usually a huge room where the animators had drawing boards set up, and as soon as you became familiar with them, they let you wander around a bit and look at the drawings and talk to the artists (though many are so focused on their work that it's clear they'd rather not engage).

I loved being in such a hive of creativity. It's almost hypnotic to watch professional animators sketch out the characters and scenes. Their precision and devotion to the projects are beautiful. It's truly remarkable work.

———

I consider it my great privilege to have provided the voice of hundreds of animated characters. At one stage, I was going in to record two or three days a week. It reached a point where I wouldn't even know what I would be doing until I arrived at the studio. I'd just take a quick read of the script, speak with the animators or director, then spin whatever I could, straight from my imagination. It was a challenge I always reveled in doing, and it's one that I sincerely hope to return to.

My voice has always been so central to the development of my characters over the years, but voicework is an entirely unique art form. People might think you have to do away with subtlety, but you don't. A voice can offer so much nuance. You can't be shy about it; you have to present in a way that demands that the audience listens. It requires a certain kind of confidence, attitude, and commitment to your character to make them special and really bring them to life.

My friend Georgia Brown is a great example of this. We worked on the 1989 animated series *Paddington Bear* together, though our friendship started when we'd been in a play together years before. We also did a separate kind of a cabaret show in the same theater where we'd done *Rocky Horror*. At one point, I started writing songs for her, too. She'd started her career out as a cabaret singer in London nightclubs like the Blue Angel. Inspired by this, I wrote a song that was what she was thinking while singing; thinking her real name was Lily Kline, I called it "A Song for Lily Kline, Who Might Have Been." But when I showed it to her, her voice got real deep and she admitted, "Actually, it was Lily Klot." Which was even better, of course.

In any case, we both enjoyed working on *Paddington Bear*. Gordon Hunt directed it, and he was of course responsible for bringing me and so many names to Hanna-Barbera. He was a genius, with a great eye and ear and sense of pushing what was possible. He was also quite an elegant man, who came off as a little austere at first but in reality, he had a real bawdy edge to him—which I loved. He appreciated naughtiness and knew he was in control of a genre that had almost limitless room to grow and become more outrageous, more enticing, and more risky with its ambitions.

Charlie Adler played the role of Paddington Bear, while I was the evil Mr. Curry. (Perhaps a bit on the nose.) He was quite good in the role; he's excellent at being cute. When we first met, I walked into the studio in my usual uniform during that era: a black shirt, black jeans, and black cowboy boots. I think the first thing he said to me was "What size shoes do you wear?"

"Um...size eight."

"Oh shit, I'm an eight and a half," he said regretfully, as though I would have otherwise taken my shoes off on the spot and passed them over to him.

We laughed about it, made fun of each other a bit, and (I believe) shared an immediate familiarity, though our backgrounds couldn't be much more different (at least on the surface). Charlie was so totally American, and I was so totally British. But we spoke the same language of imagination. While working on *Paddington*, we developed a rapport and an electricity that translated very well into all the collaborative work that would follow. We also got along well outside of the studio; we would go out all the time, to premieres and whatnot. It was all very easy and natural, never forced.

Charlie is another person who is strongly in possession of his own engine. So whenever we were in the studio together, we brought each other to very high, unlimited levels of energy and creativity. During our breaks, we'd often get a cup of coffee and stand in the stairwell; I'd smoke, Charlie would chatter away, and there was never any awkwardness. Men are often very strange about friendships, and about talking about them. That was never an issue for us. We started going out to lunch and our relationship just evolved as true friendships do. We were bros.

At the same time we were doing *Paddington*, the first part of *It* aired on television. Charlie came to work the day after he had seen it. We tended to sit next to each other because we never failed to make the other laugh, but that day he went all the way down to the other end of the table. I approached him and asked him what was up.

"I do not like you right now, and I cannot be near you," he said, looking more stern than I had ever seen him.

"What are you talking about?"

"Tim...I saw *It* last night and it's fucking freaking me out just to look at you," he said. "Please give me some space."

Safe to say, he doesn't like clowns.

We've laughed about it since—and have remained friends for nearly four decades, though when I recently asked him for an estimate, he was certain it was closer to 150 years. But back then, in our studio for *Paddington*, he was serious! He'd never watched *Rocky Horror Picture Show* or seen me in anything of the more wicked variety. He'd also never *seen* me play a villain, which is quite a different thing to hearing me be one (trust me, the bad guy from *Paddington Bear* is not quite on par with the Lord of Darkness or Pennywise). In the days that followed, once he got over it (and it really took several days), he flattered me by asking, during one of our coffee breaks, "How are you able to go from evil to the most absurd, ridiculous, insanely funny person?"

Ultimately, he got it—as I knew he would. We're both able to dive deep into the kaleidoscope of the absurd, but we each have a well of darkness within us, too. Charlie confided in me that he'd had a tough childhood, which was something I could very obviously relate to. We came to understand—though not explicitly—that as different as we very much are, we cope similarly with adversity: through humor, escapism, and extreme distraction.

As such, our childhoods informed our versatility as actors. Living through hurt, learning to navigate around it, developing a survival kit that also serves you creatively, all of that can make people much more fascinating, and better artists. A lot of people are funny but don't have the depth or expansive inner life to complement it. Others have profound recesses of pain or neglect, but don't find the channels through which it can be processed or channeled.

When Charlie started directing, I think first with *Rugrats*, that understanding between us remained much the same: silliness accompanied by trust, respect, and empathy. I'd like to believe that our work together in the genre elevated it or at least brought it to an absurd level that would resonate with all sorts of people.

Our collaboration on *The Wild Thornberrys* was a perfect example of this. The show was produced by Klasky-Csupo for Nickelodeon, and I felt privileged to pour so much of myself into the esteemed Sir Nigel Thornberry. The character was a different kind of challenge, and so delightful; of all the voice roles I've taken on, this was one of the ones that meant the most to me. I love that Nigel is so oddly naive, and he takes fatherhood so seriously and amusingly and rather sweetly. He adores his children and truly wants to be the best he can be for them, sort of like a Steve Irwin figure. I also felt deeply connected to him through our mutual love of nature and preservation, even if he was tackling the wild and I was primarily tackling weeds in my garden at home.

To this day, it makes me very hopeful how many people continue to recognize and ask me about *The Wild Thornberrys*. Nigel is perhaps the loveliest, silliest, and sweetest character to whom I've given voice.

In any case, with Charlie directing and me playing the part of Nigel, the father of the Thornberry family, we and the fabulous cast took that show—and then the feature-length film—to quite another level of absurdity. Transitioning from acting and doing voices with Charlie to being directed by him was very natural. He is a master of that craft—and the show reflects that. It has had an enduring appeal because its script (and those who gave voice to it) is very human: amusing, lucid, and dear. There's real heart there. It's also timeless, and has continued resonating with audiences of all ages ever since it first aired.

It's also worth noting that *The Wild Thornberrys* came out in an era when shows like this were no longer considered "just cartoons"; now they were "animation." In truth, it *was* less of a traditional cartoon and more of an animated series. The actors were using their real voices, not some sort of silly, cartoony voice.

As much as we could, the cast would all get into the studio together to record the scenes and really play up that family dynamic. My wife, Marianne, was played by the brilliant Jodi Carlisle; I just adored her, and found her to. be so funny and so *real*. My daughters Eliza and Debbie were played by Lacey Chabert and Danielle Harris, with whom I shared a glorious working relationship. Flea, of the Red Hot Chili Peppers, and Tom Kane were also in that cast. I wouldn't go so far as to say that we were like a real family, but we really did get along like gangbusters whenever we were in a room together.

When we were lucky enough to round up the whole ensemble into the same room, it was magic and we'd all have a blast; everyone would be constantly working off one another's energies and voices, even if there were baffled panels dividing each actor. Unfortunately, that was quite rare. I was often away working on other projects, but as soon as I returned, and especially in my scenes with Lacey, I would always try to bring as much energy as possible.

The sessions themselves were also set up with strict time limits, so it was important to use every second we could and not waste any time. Unlike when you're recording something on a live movie set or a TV show and you have a lot of time to sit around with castmates while everyone's setting up and all that, you have a designated recording session when it comes to voicework. They can go up to four hours at a time (with a break for lunch) and since the studios accommodate multiple different teams, they operate kind of like a factory, with one group coming in as soon as the one before heads out.

Still, it was a very joyful and exciting work environment for us on *The Wild Thornberrys*, however static our bodies may have been. Charlie let us play and was hysterical himself, but also patient and sweet and then ridiculous whenever we took ourselves too seriously. Which is why it worked like gangbusters.

Charlie was always zipping about, going ten thousand miles an hour, buzzing around and keeping us energized. He was also conscious of not boring us by talking or dictating *too* much as a director, which I respected. Though initially a little jarring, once you get used to it, it's undeniably thrilling to hear your director screaming with laughter and bringing all that energy to the studio.

There are a lot of different nuances in terms of the way a narrative can be interpreted, and Charlie knew, or trusted, that I would always be prepared to switch things up as needed. He was gracious about his encouragement, in a way that was highly American.

"Goddamnit, Tim! Directing you is like being a conductor, and you're a fucking Stradivarius!" he once shouted. I felt rather reinforced by his enthusiasm—however taken aback I initially was by his approach.

We worked in an open studio space, with a bunch of chairs and these easels where you could prop a script or a drawing. We'd just go to town, one-upping each other into hysterics, feeding off of each other's energy, prompting the other to tell even more outrageous stories than the one we'd just heard, or using an even more ludicrous voice to express ourselves. Then we'd go into the stairwell to have a smoke and laugh some more.

One of my fondest memories of Charlie comes from another project we collaborated on, also from Klasky-Csupo and also for Nickelodeon, a little before *The Wild Thornberrys*: a show called *Aaahh!!! Real Monsters*. It was a dark and zany show about several young monsters who go to a school underground and occasionally surface to try (and usually fail) to scare humans. It came out during what would have been the heyday of Klasky-Csupo, which was really a great, unique, scrappy little company that turned out award-winning animation. I loved being a part of it, as I never knew what was going to happen.

My character for *Aaahh!!! Real Monsters* was Zimbo, a frightening-looking wasp with (if memory serves, which it often doesn't) one leg and one tooth. I loved that one-toothed wasp. I also loved that they gave us the luxury and liberty of finding our voices. And, well, it seemed obvious to me that Zimbo should sound like a sort of Argentinian gigolo. I haven't the slightest justification for why he should sound that way, but to me, there was just no other way to play him. I came up with that voice on the fly (or on the wasp—sorry); it just shot out and Charlie ran with it. He voiced Ickis, a highly strung rabbit with enormous ears, as just pure neurosis channeled through this very odd creature.

In the studio, there was a room downstairs that had not been completely converted into a studio yet. I wasn't as much of a regular as Charlie, and one day I went in—I think it was in 1994 or so—and was told to traverse this ridiculous flight of stairs to get to a tiny room. Though really, to refer to it as a room is exceptionally generous; had there been more than two actors in there, it would have felt like a subway car during rush hour.

In fact, I believe it *must* have been just the two of us that day, because that's precisely how small the space was. For most of the episodes, the four main monsters were all together, so actors Christine Cavanaugh and David Eccles would have all been a part of it along with me and Charlie. It was just the two of us that one day, and we got in there and misbehaved so badly. We could not stop laughing at each other and at being so crammed, which in any other scenario would have just been immensely uncomfortable.

Trusting Charlie and me to pay attention to any sort of rules and essentially leaving us to our own devices to create something coherent...well, that was a decision that was not exactly well thought through. We were in hysterics before we had even left the stairwell to enter the booth.

And when I say "booth," I do mean booth—this space was essentially the size of a telephone booth. It was dark, there was no air, it was all a bit desperate, really, with the two of us flailing around a general idea about what we were meant to do and absolutely no restrictions on whatever content we produced. The result, as he would say, was a feeding frenzy. It was *preposterous*.

The tape started rolling and we were already flying, giggling like stoned teenagers. In general, Charlie and I both tend to run with whatever is thrown at us, and run quite fearlessly. We both have strong intuition, so were always one step ahead of the other, tempting each other to come up with something as bizarre as whatever had just come out of our mouths. We work the same way and are both hypersensitive to cues, and highly attuned to listen, to process, and to respond by taking it to the next level.

Sadly, I can't remember a word of the content. I just remember what a riot of a time we had improvising off each other, pushing ourselves to the absolute limits of absurdity.

———

Though maybe not with the same flair as Zimbo possessed, the characters I've animated through voicework were all touched by whimsy and a little bit of mischief. Some were vulnerable, some were just silly, but I strove to make them all approachable on some level. I always aimed to reach the same kind of multidimensional humanity as I did with physical characters. And in many ways, when behind a mic I was freer to be vulnerable, to find those different subtleties in each role, when all I had to focus on contributing was my voice.

Collaboration was always a more significant part of animation than I would have imagined. The intimacy of the voicework
setting really makes that cooperation a requisite to succeeding
within the genre. For all of my blathering about hating attention
and publicity, I absolutely gain energy from others. I like other
people. I like being around them. I can be quite introverted, but
that's usually in times of crisis. Otherwise, I'd be more inclined
to suggest I'm an extrovert (though, of course, I do reject the
notion that you can only be one or the other, as opposed to a
unique blend of the two).

I mention this here because voicework is in some ways *more*
collaborative than other kinds of acting work I've done. I never
found that the panels (which generally divide the voice actors)
got in the way of us vibing off one another, because we were
always in the same room and listening to one another, even if
we were looking at a script. Vibrationally, you're privy to everybody else's energy. It's bouncing all over the place. And that is
precisely when I found it most thrilling, because I would be that
much more inclined to up the stakes of my own part.

Once it was clear that I was well entrenched in and serious about the animation world, Marcia fielded no shortage of
voiceover requests. What show doesn't need a British villain?
Or butler? We turned down quite a lot of work during that
period—and there were some jobs I wanted but didn't get,
like the Joker in *Batman: The Animated Series*, which went to
the fabulously talented Mark Hamill—but I always jumped at
the prospect of working at Klasky-Csupo or with Charlie. We
got into a rhythm and we always had a great time. There would
never be a session that didn't tip into the bizarre, but the work
would always get done. I was proud of it. I believe he was as

well. We were brothers. I needed that in my life. As it turned out, though we drifted apart a bit professionally, he would show up quite a few years later, when I desperately needed him again.

———

As for my stint lending a voice to the *Star Wars* franchise, which is another voice that I'm still asked about with some regularity, an old friend of mine—Ian McDiarmid—had played the original in the movie, so that made the role more interesting to me, especially because he had done such a superb job. Ian and I had shared an apartment in Scotland, way back when we both worked at the Glasgow Citizens Theatre. He's Scottish; he was the original Emperor, and rather brilliant. So I had to sound a bit like him, which wasn't too hard because I knew him so well.

I was the voice of Chancellor Palpatine, also known as Darth Sidious, in a few episodes of the television version of *Star Wars: The Clone Wars*. I was a bit daunted by it, actually, because Ian had been so good in the part and was quite in my head. So that was a bit of a distraction. It was also a vocal challenge. I'm thrilled that I did it, however. I understand that it's a great honor. But I can't say that I had ever been a big *Star Wars* fan before I got cast. Even after I got cast and made myself familiar with the whole trajectory of the epic story, I never quite grasped the intensity of fans' devotion. I suppose a better way of explaining it is that I was never particularly taken with it, if I'm being honest.

No matter the production—and there were more than I can count, in quite a short span of time—it has been a true blessing to have voicework as a passion, a vocation, and an option that remains in my life. But after spending a while in the studio, I did miss performing for an audience, and felt very eager to return to the stage.

What can I say? I crave variety. I wanted to sink my teeth into a production.

Luckily for me, the world of animation was not going anywhere, and I still had a royally spectacular theater experience on my horizon.

Chapter Twenty

"There's Gonna Be a Spanking Tonight..."

(*Spamalot*)

IN THE EARLY 2000S, ERIC IDLE AND I BOTH LIVED IN LOS Angeles, so we saw each other quite a bit. One day, he called me to gauge my interest in a new musical he'd written, based on the beloved film *Monty Python and the Holy Grail.* The musical spoof would be named *Spamalot*, which I thought was hilarious. And, knowing Eric, I trusted it would be.

That said, I was a bit skeptical that the whole thing would come together and make it all the way to the stage, but Eric worked tirelessly to make it happen. It helped in no small measure that the legendary Mike Nichols signed on as the director.

From the start, he did a very smart thing, which was to invite those who he envisioned would make up the best cast to come to New York and sit around a table and just read the script with one another. Those readings ended up serving as a series of auditions.

I was asked to read for King Arthur. Mike was amused that I opted to use what I refer to as my Buckingham Palace voice for the character. It's an accent that has come in handy over the years—it's a bit lazy, as I feel I use it rather often, but it has its own energy (you can particularly hear it with phrases like *"ray-ound and about"*). An open reading with other characters is my favorite type of audition—and it went spectacularly well.

In the end, I was cast in a lead role, alongside Hank Azaria, Sara Ramirez, David Hyde Pierce, and Christian Borle, among several other superb actors. In particular, I adored Sara, who played our Lady of the Lake. I thought they were stunning, and funny, and a great singer who really knew who they were. I guess the producers of *Grey's Anatomy* picked up on that, too. I wasn't surprised in the slightest when I saw that they'd landed a role on that show, since I always considered them a star.

Especially as a British man, taking on the role of King Arthur was a bit daunting: Graham Chapman had already played him brilliantly in the movie and was quite beloved by the Pythons. I wanted to do him justice, because I so admired his performance. I had also always loved the Pythons; I used to watch them on television almost religiously as a teenager. They were so adolescent with some of their humor, yet so brilliantly funny. I gathered through Eric that their process as a group was to come together, write everything down, and all fight over what would stay in and what wouldn't. They had a curious, competitive relationship with one another. But they are all enormously funny and very interesting people.

Spamalot wasn't a Python venture, however—it was just Eric's project (though classic bits, which a lot of people in the audience would know by heart, are woven in throughout the script). It was quite interesting to play for mixed crowds, with hardcore fans who would anticipate bits coming and already be laughing or cheering for sketches they knew so well, blended in with first-timers who were taken by surprise at every turn.

Spamalot marked a real turning point in my life. It was a time of triumph and of no shortage of turbulence. Living in New York again and the sheer responsibility of the role weighed on me. But I loved the production and I grew very close with both Eric and, in time, with Mike Nichols. I just loved him and truly respected him, as a director and a friend. He always expected that I would deliver my performance consistently, an expectation of which I was very aware. But he also looked out for me and had his eye on me in a different way—which is to say that he felt growing concern for my well-being, and not for no reason.

Mike and I had a lot of dinners together, and he talked to me as an equal. He saw me as one, and he was right to. Which is perhaps pompous. But I think I deserved to be treated that way, and I don't think it would have occurred to him to treat me any other way—but he could certainly be very dismissive of actors when he wanted to be.

Before taking the show to Broadway, we headed to Chicago to do a preview period and test out the material. I remember just after we started rehearsing, there was somebody up in the flies—high above the stage, where there are several narrow walkways, and where pieces of scenery are held on ropes—who dropped something or missed the cue or made some kind of terrible noise.

Mike asked, in a rather commanding tone, "What is your name?"

Whatever his name was, we all knew he wasn't going to be there the next day. And he was not.

He was pretty old-school, Mike. He liked being known as a legend, and he undoubtedly was one. He explicitly sought out the great big beating heart that would really add an extra dimension to the show, usually one that you might not expect. That also makes any of his productions infinitely more interesting to play. That ethos was also very influential for Eric, I believe.

Anyways, once we got to Chicago, we'd rehearse and then play for five weeks and do a fair amount of tweaking along the way. Around Thanksgiving, we took the Wednesday before off, and on Thanksgiving Day, Eric rewrote Act II. I mean he *completely* restructured it and put an enormous amount of work into doing so while we were all eating stuffing and pie. That first version was very bit-focused, and Eric was determined to maintain a strong narrative throughout the production, from start to finish—which, ultimately, he pulled off quite well.

We rehearsed the new version on Friday, performed it for backers on Saturday, got on a plane on Sunday, and started technical rehearsals by Monday. It was truly the most dazzling rewrite I've ever seen. When we first played it, Mike came back to my dressing room and said, "What do you think?"

"Well, now I'm driving a Ferrari," I told him.

Of course, some of the other actors were very grumpy. There will always be grumpy actors. Several beloved scenes (like the

"She turned me into a newt!" witch scene) were left on the cutting-room floor, but if you ask me, it was only to the play's benefit. Mike was very smart about what worked and what didn't and how to shape the show.

That's not to say I didn't adore some of the material that didn't make it all the way to the audience. There was a great song called "A Spanking" that never got into the play but would have been in the movie (which Mike had wanted to make). The song stems from a scene in the original *Holy Grail*, where Arthur and his knights end up in this castle with a whole gaggle of seventeen-year-old virgins. One of the Pythons suggests a spanking. "A spanking! A spanking! There's gonna be a spanking! There's gonna be a spanking, *toniiiiiiight!*" I would have loved for that to have made it into the play, particularly because the entire company, women and men, all sang it with evident enthusiasm and enjoyment—but alas, it was not meant to be.

Perhaps it was a tad too louche, as *Spamalot* was certainly intended to be a family show.

Then again, no small amount gets lost in translation from the page to the stage.

Eric and Mike continued to revise the show as we went on—mostly the choreography, but some dialogue as well. By the time we got to New York, we had sort of perfected it, but I was already exhausted. The wonderful thing, however, was that Mike had made it very clear that the simpler our show was, the better it would be. An example of a complicated production might be if you're in a scene with ten people and they're all involved and you have to appeal to even just two or three of them at a time, using different strategies for each of them, and then the whole thing becomes more of a coordinated dance. Because of Mike's direction, the end result of *Spamalot* was quite straightforward, and, consequently, accessible to all.

For all the moving parts that Mike was in charge of, he never took his eye off me—especially when I needed him the most. When we had been staying in the Four Seasons Hotel in Chicago, a friend had sent me a case of wine, and I had propped it on the top of the TV in my room. Mike sometimes came by to talk to me in the evenings, and on one evening in particular, he sort of eyed the booze and started talking very pointedly about famous alcoholics that he had known. It was very evident that he was concerned that I was becoming one myself. As much as I appreciated his attention, though, I didn't go to rehab until several years later; in fact, at the time that he was giving me my talking-to, I felt that I had my booze intake under control.

Mike had been famous for a long time by this point, and he'd worked with just about everybody. If he hadn't, then he at least knew of them, so his list of famous alcoholics was rather exhaustive. Born in Berlin, he was a Polish Jew whose real name was Igor Mikhail Peschkowsky. "Mike Nichols" was an invention—but due to his earlier successes in the comedy scene, he had to keep it going. We had a special relationship compared to the ones he had with the other actors, but we were always careful to keep it professional on set.

Finally, we made it to our 2004 opening on Broadway. I felt profoundly privileged to work with Mike, who gave kind but pointed feedback. Every note that one ever gets from him is preceded by "That was wonderful, just wonderful. I only had one small thought..." After offering actors some general encouragement, he'd always deliver a tiny piece of completely accurate criticism that would lodge into their brain like a little arrow. That was part of his genius.

Initially, I broadly performed King Arthur's role as pantomime, or something close to vaudeville. Mike's first and recurring note to me was "Yes, that's great Tim, that's very funny and everything...now let's make it *true*." Essentially, he wanted the pureness of Arthur to emerge. The realness of the man. He wanted the audience to fall in love with Arthur for his strength and his absurdity and his weakness. And in doing so, he discharged me of the responsibility I'd felt to always be funny. I instantly understood how much more interesting it would be to make him human than to try to squeeze a giggle out of every moment. Overall, the process of developing King Arthur's character, with Mike's direction, was brilliant for regaining my stage confidence and remembering what it was like to command an audience's attention.

Playing the truth of any person requires the universal compassion that has been addressed throughout this book: No matter the genre, you have to understand your characters and play them as real people. King Arthur was a very good person, and though built into his character is the fact that he's kind of a twit, I connected with him. He has a central charm that made him such a wonderful character to play. He also asks very funny, childish questions—and by now, you should know that I mean that as a high compliment.

———

As far back as *The Rocky Horror Show*, as soon as I walk out of a stage door after a performance, my instinct—though this has admittedly grown stronger with time and general fatigue—has always been to just...run away.

Like an adult.

That instinct was exacerbated with the production of *Spamalot*, where there was always a large crowd of people at the stage door who would expect me to sign programs and to interact with me in some way afterward. As obnoxious as it feels to write this out, especially with the full knowledge that I have in fact been one of those people (for *West Side Story*) and should be more gracious, I found the whole process fairly impertinent.

Of course, I did it anyways—I felt I had to—but then, as quickly as I could, I would sneak off and drink half a bottle of wine. To be honest, I was rather impressed at my restraint at not boozing more than that. Not that such restraint would last terribly long. I had a riot of a time as Arthur, but was rather relieved when it was all over. I had signed a year's contract and we'd been doing eight shows each week. It was just as tiring as you might imagine, and I was a dead man at the end. Just a shell of a human being, really. I would sleep all day whenever I could, although I tried not to. It was clear I wasn't exactly in the best shape of my career.

Performing in *Spamalot* eventually took me back to London for a spell, where I got to play among other actors who shared my sense of humor and my natural preference for pace and delivery. Hannah Waddingham, whose star has now risen just like Sara's, played my Lady of the Lake on the West End, although I didn't bond with her quite like I'd done with Sara, partially because we weren't surrounded by the crucible of figuring out a brand-new show together and partially because...

well, a room of Brits is always going to be more reserved than a room of Americans.

There was also less of the fan presence when we were there, by which I mean the seats were still filled, but it felt as if they were newcomers to the show. The audiences were just as warm, enthusiastic, and welcoming as they'd been on Broadway, but they felt more reactive than breathlessly anticipating each and every moment. I appreciated it, honestly, since it felt like I was under less pressure. (And stage door culture wasn't really a thing on the West End at the time.) We played in London for a relatively limited run, just a few months, before Simon Russell Beale took over the throne.

It was absolutely time. I had been playing King Arthur for years and, once again, longed for a new challenge. Musicals are also much more physically demanding than many other types of performance, and I'd suffered from quite an annoying foot injury that bothered me throughout much of my tenure with *Spamalot*.

By the end, it was no surprise that those tired, itchy feet were ready to return to my garden in Los Angeles.

Chapter Twenty-One

Rosencrantz and Guildenstern Are Dead

A S YOU NOW KNOW, I'VE ENJOYED TAKING RISKS WITH MY
roles. Though it's not exactly defusing a bomb, putting one-
self out there as a performer does involve a willingness to take
chances. There have been stages when I've taken something on
particularly because I haven't felt certain that I could pull it off;
that was part of the thrill and, somehow, worked out for me
consistently.

Of course, there's nothing quite as sweet as the payoff when
you force yourself into uncomfortable territory and emerge triumphant. But you should not enter the arena at all unless you
are as prepared to fail, dramatically, as you are to succeed. That

is the perilous thing about creative risk: there's always a chance you might fall over.

I had been so lucky for most of my career; even when I felt like I was teetering on the edge, I could typically get through it.

However, in my most humbling, devastating professional experience, I fell flat on my face.

You'll note that I share this experience with brevity, but would be extremely remiss to skip over it, as to know the whole story of my creative life requires that you also know about the most humiliating moment of my career. I'm not sure I've quite recovered yet, but I will try to relay it in the most unflinching manner possible.

———

There is an annual theater festival in a place called Chichester, a seaside town in England. One of the plays they decided to revive in 2011 was Tom Stoppard's *Rosencrantz and Guildenstern Are Dead*. For this run, Trevor Nunn would be the director, and Stoppard personally recommended me to be the Player—an extravagant character. I was chuffed that he would put me forward, and very much wanted to do right by him.

The long and short of what followed (and I am going to stick with the short) is that I could not retain a word of it. I just could not learn the lines, no matter how much I tried. I cannot explain it, but I despaired of it. Eventually, the director took the book away and insisted that I wear earbuds for the production, so that somebody—in this case Liam, a friend who became my assistant—could read the dialogue into my ears, a line or two ahead. It might seem like this is somehow easier, but in reality, it is a very difficult method to attempt to navigate, because it means that you can never be purely in the moment onstage. In the end, I managed to pull it off, just barely—meaning that I was able to get from the beginning to the end of the script in one piece. But it took the heart and authenticity out of my performance—which is unacceptable (to me, at least). Neither critics nor the audience seemed to notice, but I sure did. As did the producers.

It did not take long for them to ask to see me in their office. I vividly recall walking there with Liam, feeling a bit like I was trying to walk through water, filled to the brim with dread. I knew what was coming.

"I think they're going to fire me," I told him.

"Nonsense! They can't do that. They wouldn't dare," he insisted, doing his best to reassure me.

Shortly after I had walked in, they did just that, gently informing me that "We want to ask you to withdraw."

"You're firing me?" I asked. My directness threw them off a little.

"Th-there's a car outside waiting to drive you to London."

"Well, you've thought of everything!" I said in a huff. "Sure, I'll withdraw."

With a flushed face and a quickly beating heart, I packed up my stuff in the dressing room as quickly as I could, got in the car, and was driven back to my hotel in London.

The despair I felt was unlike anything I'd ever fallen to professionally. I was gutted. And I mean utterly devastated. I had *never* been fired from a performance before, not in forty years of consistent work across several distinct parts of the entertainment industry. I spent days playing it over again and again in my head, unable to quite believe that it was real. The sting felt that much more acute because I was so convinced that I *could* have succeeded eventually, if not for their intervention.

I suppose it was quite valuable and interesting because it was such a disaster. I mean a real low point. I just could not get it out of my head that I could have made the performance better had they only had a modicum more faith in me. But I also didn't really blame them; I knew I had given them no reason to have that faith.

Thankfully, I had one or two very good friends in London who were also actors, who totally got it, and got me, and who were very supportive and helped me get out of my slump. With their encouragement, and a fair amount of time to think my way through it, I finally reached the point where I decided, "You know what? *Fuck it.*"

Though I tried to follow through with that resolve and thinking, the span that followed was very bleak. Unbeknownst to me at the time, *Rosencrantz and Guildenstern* would be my last attempt at the theater, though I was also involved in a few workshop performances of a table reading for Eric Idle's *What About Dick?* with people like Eddie Izzard, Billy Connolly, and Tracey Ullman. It was quite a funny parody, playing off of British nostalgia movies like *Remains of the Day*, but told from the point of view of a piano. Eric had a keen appreciation for those classics. Dick was a jolly adolescent who was very much admired by my character, the Reverend Whoopsie. I suppose that put me back on a stage for a time, but it wasn't a traditional performance—I think we just workshopped the show two or three times. There were no stakes.

Though I did manage to crawl out of that despondency post–*Rosencrantz and Guildenstern*, my self-confidence about performing never really returned. Even if I had been offered a role in another play around that time, I would have had to say no.

It's almost amusing now, that back in 2011, I thought that my being fired from *Rosencrantz and Guildenstern* somehow represented rock bottom for me.

I had no idea how much further down I was about to fall.

———

The following year, 2012, I had a serious stroke. It was very peculiar, and not for the reasons one would assume. I did not fade to black. I did not even feel out of sorts, or like something was very wrong. In fact, I had no idea that anything was off at all.

I remember it was a Friday, and I was receiving a massage at the time.

"Are you all right? What's happening to you?" the masseur asked, sounding concerned. I'm still not sure what tipped him off, but it was enough to make him speak up.

"I feel fine," I responded.

"Well, you don't seem fine. I'm going to call an ambulance," he insisted.

"Don't do *that*!" I exclaimed. I started thinking maybe I did feel a little out of sorts, but still thought he was being quite dramatic and over the top. I would be fine; I always ended up fine.

I probably owe my life to the fact that he ignored me, went with his instinct, and called an ambulance. Even as they were loading me in, I still thought my masseur had overreacted, and that we were going through a ridiculous and unnecessary exercise. Since I had begrudgingly agreed, I asked the ambulance to take me to Cedars-Sinai, which I had in mind as the best in the town. But after taking my vitals, the EMTs started making more commotion, sped up, and took me right to Kaiser Permanente, the closest hospital. I was not thrilled about that, but it ended up being to my great fortune: there was an incredible brain surgeon there who was able to operate on me relatively quickly. By that point, I still didn't know what was going on or what else was going to happen, which was very frightening.

And then I did, at last, fade to black.

They put me under for a major brain surgery, which is called a craniectomy. It turned out that my brain was inflamed enough, or filled with enough blood, that bone from my skull had to be removed and implanted into my abdomen to keep my brain, and me, alive. Thankfully, the operation was successful (which was by no means guaranteed). When I emerged from the hospital, I had to wear a sort of protective helmet, as my brain was literally exposed to the elements. It really wasn't my best look, but at least there was not an abundance of people looking at or judging me.

Only after the surgery was completed was I informed that I had suffered a serious stroke, which sent blood clots to my brain, two of which had been removed. Biologically, such clots really clog up the works—in other words, you're not getting sufficient blood flow, so your brain isn't receiving the oxygen and such that it needs. If there was anything impressed upon me in the aftermath, it was just how remarkable it was that I was still alive. I don't know whether I was able to respond aloud at that stage; all I can truly remember thinking was "But I didn't feel…anything."

That is not uncommon for people who suffer right-side strokes, which was the case with me. But gaining that knowledge did not bring me comfort.

When the stroke damage is on the right side, that informs the left side of the body. Luckily, I didn't suffer from a speech stroke, but it was a paralytic one, which is why I am no longer able to use half of my body. Honestly, I still feel very grateful that it was not a speech stroke, as losing the ability to be verbal and use words would have been devastating for me. Even as it was, I went through several weeks of being unable to speak, which is hell for anyone, let alone a career actor. Recovering from such major brain surgery and other effects of my condition will do that to a person, though, and I was assured that language would come back with time.

Shortly after the doctor said the word "stroke," my mind immediately flashed to my father and the stroke he had suffered when he was forty-five. Though he did not die from it, it had left him depleted, and he was hospitalized for several weeks before eventually succumbing to pneumonia. During that time, he had communicated with my mother by blinking his eyes for yes and no, a detail she shared with me many years later.

Lying there in the hospital, I realized I was now twenty-two years older than he had been when he died. The grim symmetry of our diagnosis was startling. I had no idea whether I was going to die on that slab (if you will). It seemed that it was as much of a possibility as it had ever been.

I do recall having the thought that, at sixty-seven, I was too young to be facing mortality. It wasn't something I'd dwelled on all that much. I had when I was twelve and lost my father, of course. I didn't know where he might have gone. But my inquiry basically stalled out with that question. Mortality is astonishing. We're here today and gone tomorrow. That's not scary to me, per se; it's just baffling.

I am not frightened of death. People often balk when I say that, but I do not believe that a heaven or a hell awaits me, or anything in between, though I would be curious to visit either. I gather they would be populated with plenty of fellow vaga-bonds. Without belief in some hereafter, though, what is there to be frightened about? I had been very scared when I did not know what was happening to me, because I had no sense of whether tremendous pain was forthcoming. But if death comes for me peacefully and I fade gently from light into dark obliv-ion, why would I be afraid of it? Sometimes, I rather think it would be a comfort.

I can say that now, because it's been over a dozen years, which is a sufficient amount of time to be able to reflect back calmly, and perhaps with a healthy dose of disassociation. At the time, if I'm being honest, I was just astonished to be lying there.

I do not know when exactly paralysis set in; initially, it just felt very strange that the left side of my body had gone numb. I had the stroke on a Friday, spent the weekend at Kaiser, and then I was moved by ambulance to Cedars-Sinai, where Marcia could place me under an alias to protect my identity and prevent any sort of publicity. I believe I was there for months, but the facilities blend together in my mind. When you're laid up in that kind of a state, spending much of your time staring at the ceiling or trying to grapple with being unable to use half of your body, you don't really distinguish the varied decor.

After regaining consciousness, I could comprehend words but they did not register or settle without effort. Life was exceedingly dull, monotonous, and uncertain for a long while. I was aware of where I was, but it took me a while to fully accept what had happened, as I imagine is the case with many people getting over a stroke and brain surgery. My skull had been smashed in to save my life. That's plenty to process. I needed the rest and slept a lot.

Marcia, my darling friend Cindy, and Charlie Adler were essentially the first three people by my side. My nieces also arrived at some point. Charlie really showed up throughout my recovery period, too—which was an act of great kindness and a bit of a surprise, as there were other people with whom I was closer at that stage in my life. But it seems they were more of the fair-weather variety. People in my life that should have been there for me retreated into the shadows. Marcia, Cindy, and Charlie: those three were my constants, at least for that year, when I needed them most. They have helped piece together much of that muddled span, because I was so thoroughly anesthetized, literally and then emotionally, for a time. (It would be quite something to remember brain surgery, but I'd put myself forward as the man to try.)

Marcia managed to keep my stroke from the press—not an easy feat anywhere, but especially not in LA, where celebrities are being so closely watched and monitored. I was rather unrecognizable at the time, but it's still truly remarkable that she succeeded in keeping my condition under wraps for an entire year, giving me the time and space to focus on getting back to myself.

Meanwhile, I was living in a fog. I looked frightful, and I couldn't speak clearly for ages. That part was exceptionally frustrating, because thoughts were forming again, but articulating them was such a monumental stretch. I felt like there was a massive gulf between my mind and what emerged from my mouth. Half sentences here or there would make it, but it took a while—which amounted to a whole lot of time dwelling in my own head. Being unable to string together and clearly deliver a sentence was absolute misery for somebody who values words and conversation as much as I do.

I try to avoid complaining *too* much. (I prefer doing it just enough.) But I do have the material: as I write this I'm confined to a wheelchair, having never managed to walk again. I am also currently carrying an aneurysm around in my abdomen (a tale for the next book, perhaps), with no certainty of if or when it might rupture ... *such* a tease. Even so, whining is a fucking bore for everybody involved—and it's highly unproductive. I'd rather spend my time focusing on other things.

The different ways that people cope with pain is quite interesting. I do not consider it an act of tremendous courage or bravery that I resort to humor in moments of great discomfort. It's just my go-to. I am sure it's partially a survival skill I developed a very long time ago, to the extent that humor can be developed. I'm more inclined to think that most people have some form of humor, or some ability to be amused, and the very saddest among us have had it snuffed out of them. I'm nowhere near there yet.

These are the variety of answerless questions and musings I was able to linger on for all those months that I spent waiting for my brain and skull to restore themselves. Nothing seemed too important. I thought about my childhood, and also about my father, much more than I would have imagined. Doing so was a mixed bag. I loved the opportunity to recover and dwell on the memories I still had of him, but I dwelled too much on thinking about his death and how it was handled by my mother. This would inevitably lead me down more than a rabbit hole; it would slide me into a veritable warren of thoughts I'd prefer to leave behind.

———

Once stabilized, I spent a short stint at a rehabilitation center in Beverly Hills, which was quite lovely. Then I moved to another rehab, where the real exercises began: to retrieve my ability to speak clearly, to work on smiling and facial expressions, and to try using my hand and adapting to my new normal. My bed had wheels, and one of the nurses there—a quite brawny, lovely woman—occasionally would push me out of the double doors and whizz me around the garden, just so I could get some fresh air and enjoy the courtyard.

Charlie visited quite often and one time offered to do the same, to get me outside into the sun and out of my room for a bit. To do so required that I put on a whole sort of body of armor. I vividly recall one day, among a sea of gray ones that otherwise blend together, when it was just the two of us. It was very quiet, which is a rare state for the two of us to be in: generally, we collectively suck all the oxygen out of a given room. But for whatever reason, this day was very easy, gentle.

He was washing his hands in the sitting area where there was a mirror. I gave him a rather crooked smile, I'm sure, and told him that I was looking at one of the world's best cheerleaders. He got quite emotional, which was a little much, and I made some quip to snap him out of that. I *am* still British, after all.

My mind was growing sharper by the day, or so I was told by my visitors, particularly Marcia, Charlie, and my nieces. I could feel it as well. On the wall of the facility were various paintings, from end to end. They were very basic prints from famous artists, so I wasn't jumping through any miraculous mind hoops, but I found myself able to identify a lot of the artists, which my niece Kate and Charlie both made quite a big deal about. I suppose it gave some evidence that I was still present, still in my mind, still capable of looking at art and recognizing it.

It was perhaps on the same journey when we then passed a big photography exhibit. Charlie was pushing my wheelchair, looking ahead. I recognized the actress and comedian Imogene Coca, who was in a photograph with, I think, Sid Caesar.

"Stop!" I shouted (though it was likely more of a slurred murmur).

"Who is that?" Kate asked.

"That's Imogene Coca. Charlie's great buddy. They played together." I spoke about it for probably a minute, with full memory of their relationship and without too much trouble articulating it. I was speaking slowly, but I didn't have to think before I spoke. I suppose those moments of recognition signaled that I was going to come back. In some form. The fact that I could retrieve those details felt like hope—to me and to those around me. Incrementally, week to week, parts of my brain were firing back up. I noticed that I was finding humor in little details, just snippets of conversations that would make me sort of chuckle again.

Humor helped me get back to myself, and it happened very naturally. (I've nicknamed my left hand, the one I can't use anymore, Teddy. Something about considering it as a wholly separate entity has helped me think of it with care and compassion rather than frustration.) This world can quickly veer into being a very boring place, a very cynical place, a very twisted place, depending on where you train your gaze and what you choose to absorb. I cannot imagine I would still be alive, nor would I want to remain living, if I didn't have immediate access to humor and absurdity. That capacity never left me, and for that I am endlessly grateful.

Of course, it was still a rather brutal time, with cycles of people jabbing and manipulating my body for months, and my not being able to fully grasp precisely what was going to come of all of it, and not knowing when or if I would be back in the comfort of my home. After decades of jumping from one thing to the next, all I really wanted to do was be firmly rooted back in my own space.

When the time came, we tried to make my home suitable for my condition. It was retrofitted with ramps for the stairs and had an electric chair installed. I quite enjoyed that, actually, but it got to be too much because it was a multilevel house. Even when using my little travel wheelchair, I couldn't fit into the powder room downstairs, which was the *only* downstairs bathroom and thus rather problematic.

I loved that home and those gardens so much and had poured so much of myself into it over the years. It was a terribly hard decision to move away from there. But the inconvenience just proved to be too much.

Packing up and moving onward is what I do.

I love the distinct eccentricities of each and every home I've lived in over the years; I've adapted to new homes, and then adapted them to me. In one of them, there were two buttons underneath a desk that opened to a bar and a human-sized safe, with stairs inside that went down to a wine cellar. But, of course, not all eccentricities need be quite so extravagant—and it's most important that a house fits the life you lead.

Leaving to find a new, one-story home helped me accept that my life was going to be quite different from now on. After a short stay at a rental, I bought my current house. I did some extensive renovations to open it up as much as possible. I tried to be true to the period in which it had been built, by restoring it with kind of fifties decor...but I'd also lived through the 1950s, and I hated it. So I ended up having my favorite furniture delivered, deciding on the colors for the walls (red for the dining room, green for the guest room), and have done everything I can to make it work for me.

As for the garden, well—I'm gearing up to do quite a bit more out there. Over the years, I've read a lot of gardening books and visited some beautiful spaces all over the world, from the Chelsea Physic Garden in London to the Jardin Majorelle of Marrakesh. I've always enjoyed the planning and research part of bringing a garden to life. Perhaps I might add in some formal hedging and make it more mysterious, like a labyrinth. Or build a cozy cabana at the end of the garden, surrounded by jasmine so it smells sweet and fresh. There'd be a bar, of course, and maybe a jungle of some sort. There might even be banana trees.

Until I make a decision, I'll let my imagination run wild.

My life has changed dramatically in just about every way, especially from the outside looking in. After an extremely fortuitous stretch of decades without ever being out of work for more than three or four months at a time, the roles I can now take are almost exclusively voicework. I did appear as the criminologist in the *Rocky Horror Picture Show* remake in 2016, which was a curious experience. The character is staring into the camera, so they included a teleprompter as a courtesy, but I didn't need it. I suppose it added a bit of extra security, however.

I also participated in a live-streamed *Rocky Horror Picture Show* on Halloween 2020, just prior to the United States' presidential election, in support of the Wisconsin Democrats. I was able to reprise my role as Frank and revisit a few of my favorite scenes almost fifty years later, which is something I never thought I'd be able to do. Barry Bostwick and Nell Campbell were also involved, and it was lovely working with them again, even if only virtually, and only for one night. I would have done just about anything I could to ensure Donald Trump's defeat that November. The less said about him, the better. I had my lines in front of me for that, too. I would be terrified to take on a role onstage, though, which in itself is quite upsetting.

There have been other serious downsides from the stroke, too. I fear I have a shorter temper now, which gets vocalized in a way that it never would have before. Being handled by caregivers can also be very painful, particularly on my left side, which is super sensitive. But for the most part, I've been enormously lucky with the help I've received. The same guys have been with me for over a decade, and I am very thankful for their constant care.

My short-term memory is also blown. That remains very frustrating, and adapting to that has been tough, but I've gained a new relationship with my long-term memory, which is pretty spot on. The examined life and all that. It wasn't something I had practiced before the stroke. I was always a forward-thinker;

I never wanted to return to my childhood home, or to the stages, sets, and studios of my past. But it has been surprisingly, strangely healing. And given the restrictions of my present state, sometimes a tour through my memory is the only adventure available.

For all that's changed, there are many ways that my persuasions have not changed a bit. I still enjoy gardening; I've just taken on more of a director role. I still feel most at ease when I'm chatting with dear friends, socializing, and having a few drinks—although I don't overdo it anymore. My humor's still intact, I still despise bullies, and I still cherish language.

I've dabbled with every variety of attitude about my lot in life, and consistently land on the "bright side of life." For yourself and for anybody you're with, it's dull and annoying to dwell in total darkness. Without mischief, without charm, without laughter, you're no fun to be or to be around.

As for the future—it's a highly uncertain place for me, which is how I prefer it. My discomfort and disability notwithstanding, I hope to perform again. To fall in love again. To experience the full spectrum of human emotion and experience. To spend as much time as I can with my good friends, people I love, people who love me. It's the luckiest thing about living. It's extraordinary how many people go without it. All the Eleanor Rigbys.

If life and all its mischievous left turns—which I do excel at executing—has offered me anything, it's that guarantees are but an illusion. Contracts can be shredded, crystal balls can be shattered, willpower can overturn the grimmest presumptions.

Today, I am feeling quite strong. My rough patches have been rough, but I've survived them all. That confidence has been to my detriment at times, but overall, it has served me well. I've been given awfully dire diagnoses with some regularity since the stroke. But plenty of doctors, and perhaps even I, have underestimated my staying power.

I've had more than one staring contest with Death, and it has eventually blinked first.

This is a big reason why I've come to believe—or at least to happily convince myself—that I can survive anything. Like some kind of toad. (I don't know if toads can survive anything, but I believe they're quite hardy and would fare well in their fair share of disasters.) Maybe a dinosaur is a better analogy. Except they didn't survive anything. Though they had a good run, I suppose, and some of them turned into birds.

I wouldn't mind turning into a bird.

Conclusion

Now What?

Despite my itchy feet and vagabond heart, I don't really travel much anymore. I do visit the occasional fan conventions, however, which can be interesting, surprising, flattering, exceptionally strange, and at times quite touching.

One of the most busy and memorable major conventions that I've attended was in Toronto in 2017. Charlie moderated a talk for me; over the years, he's done so for a few panels and Q&As and made it easier for me to navigate them with confidence. For somebody so full of energy, he's quite patient with me. He knows my rhythm well enough to read when I need more time, when it would be best for him to step in, and when I'm done.

There were thousands and thousands of people there, enough to startle me and make me quite nervous about the whole thing. I was in my wheelchair, it was very crowded, and it takes a lot out of me to maintain my energy for extended periods of time like that, especially onstage. It's very important to me to show dignity, gratitude, and respect toward everybody who bothers to attend.

The Q&A section at that Toronto convention was an infusion of hope. The range of people who came down the aisle to ask questions was astonishing to me, to Charlie, and even to my caretaker, Ramon. Most walks of life were present: every gender and mixed gender, with attendees who had brought their seven- and eight-year-old kids along, and others who looked like they were pushing one hundred years old. Costumes were on full display, with people dressed as Transylvanians, as punk rockers, as pirates. Mozart to Muppets, clowns to kings. It was humbling, and not just a little surreal, to look out and see much of my life's work reflected in people who were still interested in what I had to say.

Everybody spoke with respect and—dare I say—a kind of reverence about my work that I found so generous. People seemed delighted that they were being listened to, no matter what they looked like or who they were. Which was such an honor, given that I certainly did not look like I once did. My speech is halting and at times I still struggle to find my words. But none of that mattered. I accepted them for whoever they were, I respected their questions, took them seriously, and did my best to amuse them. It never loses its power to have these incredibly nervous kids approach and tell me that I have changed their life in one way or the other. Those exchanges are so meaningful to me. I'm truly grateful for them. And for you.

There have been some impossibly long, dark nights when I thought that I would never be able to engage with audiences again. But it's these moving encounters with fans over the years that ultimately convinced me to stop and take the time to share my story. The notion that my experiences might resonate helps me persevere—if they strike a chord with only that one teenager, alone with a book in his room, as I so often was; or that young woman reading this on an interminably long bus ride; or that older queen, hopefully still in his fishnets, who saw *Rocky*

Horror upstairs at the Royal Court; or that middle-aged mother who organizes *Clue* watching parties and refuses entry to anybody out of costume; or that buttoned-up bank clerk who relishes musicals; or that woman who kicked me out of the Waverly for being myself.

Or you.

More than anything, I hope this book resonates with you.

And I can only hope that you will take away a sound belief that—if you're searching for where you belong—you always have a home within yourself. If the past dozen years have taught me anything, it's that being a vagabond is not defined by distance traveled or the number of places I've called home; it's about adopting a certain attitude toward life.

Much like a painter might consider what to do with a blank canvas, or a gardener with a blank space in the backyard, a vagabond looks upon the world as a field of potential and possibility, where beauty can be not just found but created—and adventure awaits any and all who are willing to seek it out.

Acknowledgments

I AM A VERY LUCKY MAN, ONE WHO HAS BEEN GIVEN UNFATH-omable opportunities. The task of thanking all those who have made those chances possible is not merely daunting—it is impossible. Though this list is by no means complete, I feel an extra debt of gratitude to the following people, who have been directly involved in enabling me to impart my story.

To my dedicated manager and dear friend **Marcia Hurwitz**, who encouraged this endeavor and so many others over the course of our decades of adventure;

To my nieces and nephew, **Kate**, **Julia**, and **Mark**, for their love and support;

To my collaborator and confidante, **Domenica Alioto** (who believes I'm smarter than I am), who never fails to lift my spirits, who brings hope and laughter with every visit, and without whom this book simply would not exist;

To **Cindy Hudson**, my steadfast Nashville belle, for being an endless source of support through many seasons of ups and downs;

To **Jon Michael Darga**, my enthusiastic agent, who never gave up on making this book a reality;

To **Carrie Napolitano**, **Ben Schafer**, the entire team at Hachette Book Group, and to my publishers worldwide, for believing in *Vagabond*;

To **Richard Cork**, who opened my eyes;

To **Peter Wood** and **Peter Shaffer**, for polishing my love of words by example;

To **Charlie Adler**, for the laughter and for being the world's best cheerleader;

To my bros, **Ramon Garcia**, **Martin Garcia**, and **John Susi**, for their care, patience, and willingness to put up with me;

And to **Mae Malone Alioto Howard**, my honorary niece and a true inspiration, for asking all the right questions and for wanting to be my friend.

Appendix

Production	Year	Character
A Midsummer Night's Dream	1972	Puck
Time Off? Not a Ghost of a Chance	1972	Unknown
The Rocky Horror Show	1973–1975	Dr. Frank-N-Furter
Give the Gaffers Time to Love You	1973	Unknown
Travesties	1975–1976	Tristan Tzara
Amadeus	1980–1981	Wolfgang Amadeus Mozart
The Pirates of Penzance	1982	The Pirate King
The Rivals	1983	Acres
Love for Love	1985–1986	Tattle
Dalliance	1985–1986	Theodore
The Threepenny Opera	1986	Macheath aka Mack the Knife
Me and My Girl	1987–1988	Bill Snibson
The Art of Success	1989–1990	William Hogarth
My Favorite Year	1992	Alan Swann
A Christmas Carol	2001	Ebenezer Scrooge
Spamalot	2004–2007	King Arthur
Rosencrantz and Guildenstern Are Dead	2011	The Player
What About Dick?	2012	Reverend Whoopsie

Filmography Credits

Motion Picture	Year	Character
The Rocky Horror Picture Show	1975	Dr. Frank-N-Furter
The Shout	1978	Robert Graves
Times Square	1980	Johnny LaGuardia
Annie	1982	Rooster Hannigan
The Ploughman's Lunch	1983	Jeremy Hancock
Legend	1985	Darkness
Clue	1985	Wadsworth
Pass the Ammo	1988	Rev. Ray Porter
The Hunt for Red October	1990	Dr. Petrov
Oscar	1991	Dr. Thornton Poole
Home Alone 2: Lost in New York	1992	Mr. Hector (the Concierge)
Passed Away	1992	Boyd Pinter
The Three Musketeers	1993	Cardinal Richelieu
Loaded Weapon 1	1993	Jigsaw
The Shadow	1994	Farley Claymore
Congo	1995	Herkermer Homolka
Lover's Knot	1996	Cupid's Caseworker
Muppet Treasure Island	1996	Long John Silver
McHale's Navy	1997	Maj. Vladikov
Addams Family Reunion	1998	Gomez Addams
Pirates of the Plain	1999	Jezebel Jack
Charlie's Angels	2000	Roger Corwin
Sorted	2000	Damian Kemp
Four Dogs Playing Poker	2000	Felix
Scary Movie 2	2001	Professor Oldman
Ritual	2001	Matthew Hope
The Scoundrel's Wife / Home Front	2002	Father Antoine
Kinsey	2004	Thurman Rice

Motion Picture	Year	Character
Bailey's Billion$	2005	Caspar Pennington
Christmas in Wonderland	2007	McLoosh
The Secret of Moonacre	2008	Coeur De Noir
Burke and Hare	2010	Dr. Monroe

Television Credits

Show	Year	Character
Sinking Fish Move Sideways	1968	Waiter on Train
ITV Saturday Night Theatre	1970	Crosscapel
Ace of Wands	1970	Cashier
The Duchess of Malfi	1972	Madman
Armchair Theatre: Verite	1973	Mik
Play for Today: Schmoedipus	1974	Glen
Napoleon and Love	1974	Eugene
Three Men in a Boat	1975	Jerome K. Jerome
Rock Follies of '77	1977	Stevie Streeter
Life of Shakespeare	1978	William Shakespeare
Oliver Twist	1982	Bill Sikes
Blue Money	1982	Larry Gormley
Video Stars	1983	Teddy Whazz
Ligmalion: A Musical for the 80s	1985	Eden Rothwell Esq.
The Worst Witch	1986	The Grand Wizard
Wiseguy	1989	Winston Newquay
The Tracey Ullman Show	1989	Ian Miles
It	1990	Pennywise
The Wall: Live in Berlin	1990	The Prosecutor
Big Deals	1991	Christopher Nissell
Tales from the Crypt	1993	Ma, Pa, and Winona Brackett
Roseanne	1993	Roger
Earth 2	1994	Gaal
The Naked Truth	1995	Sir Rudolph Haley
Titanic	1996	Simon Doonan
Doom Runners	1997	Dr. Kao
Over the Top	1997	Simon Ferguson
Lexx	1997	Poet Man
Jackie's Back!	1999	Edward Whatsett St. John

Show	Year	Character
The Unbelievables	1999	Vaudevillain
Rude Awakening	1999–2000	Martin Crisp
Wolf Girl aka Blood Moon	2001	Harley Dune
Attila	2001	Theodosius
Family Affair	2002–2003	Mr. Giles French
Will & Grace	2004	Marion Finster
Monk	2004	Dale "The Whale" Biederbeck
Psych	2007	Nigel St. Nigel
The Colour of Magic	2008	Trymon
Cranford	2009	Signor Brunoni
Alice	2009	Dodo
Agatha Christie's Poirot	2009	Lord Boynton
Criminal Minds	2010	Billy Flynn
TRHPS: Let's Do the Time Warp Again	2016	The Criminologist (An Expert)

Voice Credits

Voices in Film

Motion Picture	Year	Character
FernGully: The Last Rainforest	1992	Hexxus
The Pebble and the Penguin	1995	Drake
Beauty and the Beast: The Enchanted Christmas	1997	Forte
A Christmas Carol	1997	Ebenezer Scrooge
The Rugrats Movie	1998	Rex Pester
The Easter Story Keepers	1998	Nero
Scooby-Doo! and the Witch's Ghost	1999	Ben Ravencroft
Bartok the Magnificent	1999	The Skull
Lion of Oz	2000	Captain Fitzgerald
Rugrats in Paris: The Movie	2000	Sumo Singer
Barbie in the Nutcracker	2001	The Mouse King
I, Crocodile	2002	Crocodile
The Cat Returns	2002	The Cat King
The Wild Thornberrys Movie	2002	Nigel Thornberry, Radcliff Thornberry
Rugrats Go Wild	2003	Nigel Thornberry
¡Mucha Lucha!: The Return of El Maléfico	2005	El Maléfico
Valiant	2005	Von Talon
Queer Duck: The Movie	2006	Peccary
Garfield: A Tail of Two Kitties	2006	Prince
A Sesame Street Christmas Carol	2006	Narrator
The Chosen One	2007	Lucifer
Once Upon a Christmas Village	2007	Sir Evil
Fly Me to the Moon	2008	Yegor

Motion Picture	Year	Character
Scooby-Doo! and the Goblin King	2008	The Goblin King
Barbie and the Three Musketeers	2009	Philippe
Mythic Journeys	2009	The King
The North Star	2010	Narrator
Curious George 2: Follow That Monkey!	2010	Picadilly
A Turtle's Tale: Sammy's Adventures	2010	Fluffy
The Voyages of Young Doctor Dolittle	2011	Doctor Dolittle
The Outback	2012	Blacktooth
Back to the Sea	2012	Eric
Strange Frame	2012	Dorlan Mig
Gingerclown	2013	Gingerclown
Saving Santa	2013	Nevil Baddington
Axel: The Biggest Little Hero	2014	Papa Qi
Ribbit	2014	Terence
Long Drive Home	2017	Monster Head AD
Stream	2024	Lockwood

Voices in Television

Show	Year	Character
The Greatest Adventure: Stories from the Bible	1988–1989	The Serpent, Judas Iscariot
Fantastic Max	1989	Dermot D. McDermott (4 episodes)
Long Ago and Far Away	1989	Abel
Paddington Bear	1989	Mr. Curry (13 episodes)
Fox's Peter Pan & the Pirates	1990–1991	Captain Hook

Show	Year	Character
Gravedale High	1990	Mr. Tutner
The Adventures of Don Coyote and Sancho Panda	1990	Sultan
Wake, Rattle & Roll	1990–1991	Ronald Chump
Tiny Toon Adventures	1990	Prince Charles, Reginald
The Marzipan Pig	1990	Narrator
TaleSpin	1990	Thaddeus E. Klang (2 episodes)
The Pirates of Dark Water	1991–1993	Konk
The Legend of Prince Valiant	1991–1994	Sir Gawain
Captain Planet and the Planeteers	1991–1996	MAL
Darkwing Duck	1991–1992	Taurus Bulba
Tom & Jerry Kids	1991–1994	Sheriff of Rottingham, Banker (2 episodes)
Fish Police	1992	Sharkster
Defenders of Dynatron City	1992	Atom Ed
Capitol Critters	1992	Senator
Dinosaurs	1992–1994	Various roles
Wild West C.O.W.-Boys of Moo Mesa	1992	Jacque Le Beefe
Batman: The Animated Series	1992	Henchman
Liquid Television	1992	The Snake
The Little Mermaid	1992–1994	Evil Manta
The Steadfast Tin Soldier	1992	Jack-in-the-Box
Eek! The Cat	1992	Narrator
Mighty Max	1993–1994	Skullmaster, Jules Verne
Droopy, Master Detective	1993	Additional voices
Aaahh!!! Real Monsters	1994–1997	Zimbo, Additional roles
Duckman	1994–1997	King Chicken, Simon Desmond
Sonic the Hedgehog	1994	King Acorn, Keeper of the Time Stones

Show	Year	Character
Aladdin	1994	Amok Mon-Ra, Caliph Kapok
Superhuman Samurai Syber-Squad	1994–1995	Kilokahn
Turbocharged Thunderbirds	1994–1995	The Atrocimator (13 episodes)
The Mask: Animated Series	1995–1997	Pretorius
Daisy-Head Mayzie	1995	Finagle
Gargoyles	1995–1996	Dr. Anton Sevarius
Adventures from the Book of Virtues	1996	King Minos, Gessler
Quack Pack	1996	Moltoc
The Story of Santa Claus	1996	Nostros
Mighty Ducks	1996–1997	Lord Dragaunus
Bruno the Kid	1996–1997	Lazlo Gigahurtz (9 episodes)
Jumanji	1996–1998	Trader Slick
Freakazoid!	1997	Dr. Mystico
Casper	1997	Pianist
Teen Angel	1997	The Frog
Stories from My Childhood	1998	The Beast
Where on Earth Is Carmen Sandiego?	1998	Dr. Gunnar Maelstrom (3 episodes)
The Net	1998	The Sorcerer (10 episodes)
The First Snow of Winter	1998	Voley
Voltron: The Third Dimension	1998–2000	Prince Lotor, King Alfor
The Wild Thornberrys	1998–2004	Nigel Thornberry, additional voices
Hey Arnold!	1999, 2003	Leichliter
Xyber 9: New Dawn	1999	King Renard
Big Guy and Rusty the Boy Robot	1999, 2001	Dr. Neugog
Recess	1999	Dr. Slicer

Show	Year	Character
Johnny Bravo	1999	Big Brother
Pinky, Elmyra & the Brain	1999	Monkman
The Titanic Chronicles	1999	Officer Lightoller
Martial Law	2000	The One
Batman Beyond	2000	Mutro Botha
100 Deeds for Eddie McDowd	2000	The Rottweiler
Redwall	2000–2001	Slagar the Cruel
Gary & Mike	2001	Jared Wexler
Teacher's Pet	2001	Spooky
Teamo Supremo	2002–2003	Laser Pirate, Dastardly Dentist
Samurai Jack	2002	Worm 1
Ozzy & Drix	2002	Nick O'Teen, Scarlet Fever
The Adventures of Jimmy Neutron: Boy Genius	2003–2005	Professor Finbarr Calamitous
K10C: Kids' Ten Commandments	2003	Hazzaka
Chalkzone	2003	Jacko
The Proud Family	2003	Pervical
Higglytown Heroes	2004	Librarian Hero
Duck Dodgers	2005	Magnificent Rogue
Loonatics Unleashed	2005	Ringmaster
The Jimmy Timmy Power Hour 2	2006	Professor Finbarr Calamitous
Eloise: The Animated Series	2006	Mr. Salamone (13 episodes)
Phineas and Ferb	2008, 2012	Stubbings, Worthington Dubois
Ben 10: Alien Force	2008	Dr. Joseph Chadwick, Knight #2
Regular Show	2010	Hot Dog Leader, Master Prank Caller #2
Young Justice	2012–2013	G. Gordon Godfrey
Transformers: Rescue Bots	2012	Doctor Morocco

Show	Year	Character
The High Fructose Adventures of Annoying Orange	2012	Arugula, Endive, Plum
Randy Cunningham: 9th Grade Ninja	2012	The Sorcerer
Star Wars: The Clone Wars	2012	Chancellor Palpatine/ Darth Sidious
Wonder Pets	2013	Tin Man
Ben 10: Omniverse	2013	Dr. Joseph Chadwick, Stage Manager
Over the Garden Wall	2014	Auntie Whispers

Voices in Video Games

Video Game	Year	Character
Gabriel Knight: Sins of the Fathers	1993	Gabriel Knight
Wing Commander III: Heart of the Tiger	1994	Melek
Toonstruck	1996	Count Nefarious
Duckman: The Graphic Adventures of a Private Dick	1997	King Chicken
Gabriel Knight 3	1999	Gabriel Knight
Sacrifice	2000	Stratos
The Four Horsemen of the Apocalypse	2002	Satan
Scooby-Doo! Night of 100 Frights	2002	Mastermind
The Adventures of Jimmy Neutron Boy Genius	2003	Professor Finbarr Calamitous
Lemony Snicket's A Series of Unfortunate Events	2004	Lemony Snicket
Nicktoons Unite!	2005	Professor Finbarr Calamitous

Video Game	Year	Character
Nicktoons Winners Cup Racing	2006	Professor Finbarr Calamitous
Nicktoons: Attack of the Toybots	2007	Professor Finbarr Calamitous
Brütal Legend	2009	Emperor Doviculus
Dragon Age: Origins	2009	Arl Rendon Howe

About the Author

HAVEN'T YOU BEEN PAYING ATTENTION?

6419911 3R00090